THE RENOVATION MANIPULATION

THE RENOVATION MANIPULATION

The Church Counter-Renovation Handbook

by
Michael S. Rose

AQUINAS PUBLISHING LTD
CINCINNATI

Pictured on the front cover is the reredos and tabernacle at St. Francis Xavier Church in Petoskey, Michigan. As this edition was going to press this parish was embroiled in a typical renovation process. Plans called for the tabernacle to be moved into a "reservation chapel" and, according to Sister Arlene Benett, diocesan liturgist for the Diocese of Gaylord, the reredos ought to be "given to the Protestants."

Cover design by Scott Hofmann
Front cover photograph by Troy Frantz
Back cover photograph by Joe Hoffman, Jr.

Aquinas Publishing Ltd
P.O. Box 11260
Cincinnati, Ohio 45211-0260

Ad Maiorem Dei Gloriam

ACKNOWLEDGEMENTS

The author wishes to express his thanks to all those who helped put this book together, especially Barbara E. Rose, D. Grant Herring, Charles M. Wilson, R. Michael Dunnigan, Scott Hofmann, Paul Likoudis, Ian Rutherford, David Alexander, Teresa Tillotson, Lois Westerheide, and Michael T. Hendley.

FOREWORD

THERE IS NO QUESTION that the Church, especially in Europe and North America, is undergoing a terrible internal crisis. Some scholars say that it is the worst that the Church has faced since the Reformation or even the Arian heresy of the 4th century; still others say it is the worst crisis the Church has yet faced in her 2,000-year history.

Here in the United States, over the past 35 years the disaster has unfolded before our very eyes. What were once solidly Catholic institutions of higher learning have abandoned their Catholic identity. There has been a precipitous decline in vocations to the clergy and religious life. It seems that almost every day we hear of someone, even a family member, who has ceased practicing the Catholic faith or left the Church for some other religion or no religion at all. Even those who remain in the Church seem indifferent or confused over what they are supposed to believe because they hear the Holy Father saying one thing and their local clergy saying another. And these are just a few examples of the many that could be cited.

Far more damaging than the loss of institutional identity and the defections of individuals is the blurring of the nature of the summit of Catholic worship itself, the Holy Sacrifice of the Mass. Before I was received into the Church as a 30-year-old convert in 1966, I was instructed, and believed, that in the Mass the sacrifice of Calvary is repeated. Christ again offers himself through the priest, although bloodlessly. Now, in many parishes, the mention of this sacrificial character of the Mass has virtually disappeared. The prevailing notion is that Christ becomes present in the gathered community — as indeed he does — but without any reference to the sacrificial aspect of the Mass, and with the implication that somehow the community brings about our Lord's Eucharistic presence. It is therefore not surprising that folksiness has replaced solemnity, standing replaces kneeling, abandon replaces decorum, banality replaces reverence and, in general, the commonplace or the ugly replaces the beautiful.

This minimalist "less is more" approach to worship is in stark contrast to the environment that existed in the Church for centuries and which, I am convinced, the Fathers of the Second Vatican Council had no intention of changing and, to the contrary, intended to preserve. Church buildings, as we know, play a key role in creating an atmosphere conducive to worship. If this atmosphere clashes with the mood that liturgists and so-called experts wish to produce, something has to give. And give it has!

In spite of the overwhelming evidence to the contrary, there is a group that denies that there is anything seriously amiss in the Church today. They tell us that the vast majority of the faithful has enthusiastically embraced all of the changes in the liturgy. Doctrinal error and confusion are, so they say, not all that serious and are merely typical of what has followed ecumenical councils in the past. We are assured that, once the "Spirit of Vatican II" is fully implemented, a new age will dawn. This presupposition, as

Michael Rose so ably documents in this book, governs those who dictate how our churches are to be renovated to accommodate the new concept of Catholic worship. Fortunately, evidence exists that contradicts this faulty premise.

In 1984, the Saint Joseph Foundation was formed to provide professional advice and assistance to Catholics who believe that their rights to Catholic truth and authentic Catholic worship are threatened or actually violated. During the fifteen years that have followed, I have served as the Foundation's Executive Director. Since 1989 our case files have been computerized and, for the ten years between then and 1999, we have received a total of 3,668 requests for assistance, some 90% of which have originated after 1996. Of this number, 93 involved the renovation of church buildings. I have reviewed these files and can confirm that the examples Michael Rose cites in the present work are typical of what we know has occurred in dozens of parishes throughout the United States. The tactics of blatantly manipulating the faithful, demonizing and marginalizing the opposition, misrepresenting the status of "Environment and Art in Catholic Worship," fabricating the requirements of Church law and the Second Vatican Council and falsifying history are proverbial.

Another matter that ought to be mentioned is spiritual and material cost of renovations. We have only sketchy data on the former, but we have accounts in our case files of parishioners who have left parishes, stopped going to Mass or, sadly, left the Church altogether because they were so distraught over the tactics employed by the renovators. Sadly, the last words of the last canon in the Code of Canon Law, "the salvation of souls is always the supreme law of the Church" are ignored all too often.

Likewise, there is very little available financial data. However, we can make some inferences from the fact that the 1962 *Official Catholic Directory* showed that there were then 17,156 parishes in the United States. If the altars and communion rails were torn out of 75 percent of these churches, which I think is a very conservative estimate, and the cost of this destruction alone was estimated at just $10,000 per building, this means that 12,867 churches were needlessly disfigured at a total cost of $128,670,000. This does not include other unnecessary and often unwanted changes such as moving tabernacles to closet-like "chapels," building baptismal fonts that resemble swimming pools and moving choirs and organ consoles to where sanctuaries used to be. It also does not include the 2,428 parishes created between 1962 and 1998 or the older buildings that have been renovated twice. When all this is considered, I do not think an admittedly rough estimate of the dollars squandered at more than 200,000,000 is unreasonable. The cost in lost art and history is, of course, incalculable.

A final point to remember is that the renovators do not prevail against the parishioners in all cases. In some of the cases handled by the Saint Joseph Foundation, the renovations were either scaled back or stopped completely. Most certainly, the same thing happened in many instances where the Foundation was not involved. As this book shows, the Professional Church Renovators and their allies are vulnerable. A well informed, determined and united community can succeed in defending its artistic, cultural and historical treasure against them.

CHARLES M. WILSON
St. Joseph Foundation
San Antonio, Texas

CONTENTS

INTRODUCTION

Discovering the Blueprint
A pattern of controversy and discord

ಬಂಚ್ಞ

THROUGHOUT CHURCH HISTORY, architecture reflected the spiritual values of the people and the age.
The basilicas of the early Church fostered meditation
and concentration. The Romanesque inspired the search
for symbols that would lead the spirit toward God. In the
Middle Ages, intense religious fervor and intellectual vigor
led to the Gothic "Bibles in stone," followed by Renaissance
architecture, which reflected the new love for erudition,
science, and metaphysics.

The Council of Trent called for a return to the cruciform basilica plan of the early Church, since that model
was understood to be most conducive to the catechesis and
preaching it considered essential to battling the various
heresies of the day. Counter-Reformation emphases inspired the exterior and interior of Catholic churches in
North America until a few decades ago. The old masters
expressed the Catholic faith in the very birth of their art
by means of elaborate high altars and tabernacles, special
niche and aisle shrines dedicated to the Virgin Mary and

the saints, prominent pulpits for preaching, and an abundance of art in glass, sculpture or painting to teach the truths necessary for salvation. The atmosphere created on this model was one of religious mystery wherein one could experience a little of the unearthly joy of the New Jerusalem, where one's soul could meet with Christ in a unique way. Every detail, however small, had profound meaning for both artist and layman. These churches told the story of Christ and his Church, taught, catechized, and illustrated the lives of the Church's saintly souls.

In the 20th century, most scholars readily admit, the Church has not yet shown the ability to produce genuinely creative artists. While there are many skillfully-designed churches modeled on previous styles — for example, the National Shrine of the Immaculate Conception in Washington, D.C. or the Cathedral of St. Louis the King in St. Louis — 20th century Church architects have yet to produce anything that embodies a sense of the sublime, an architecture that inspires faith and belief and humbles the viewer with a power of eternal goodness, beauty and truth.

This problem is exacerbated by the contemporary church renovation movement, the roots of which extend back to the 1940's.[1] Even then, churches of previous centuries were deemed irrelevant by an elite corps of Church intellectuals and architects who would have greater influence throughout the Church in the years to come. The traditional architectural elements and furnishings were disparaged and a new model based on architectural modernism with its cold and hard lines, its starkness and over-emphasis on utility was born. The post-war building boom saw the construction of numerous Catholic churches as parishes grew and the Church greatly increased in numbers throughout North America. The churches built in this

---

[1] Pope Pius XII responded effectively to some of the archi-liturgical trends that were being promoted in the 1940's through his encyclical on the liturgy, *Mediator Dei*, released in 1947.

brief era were diverse in their designs, but many were obviously disconnected with the tradition of Catholic architecture, reflecting more a Protestant or secular influence.

The Second Vatican Council gave these architects and intellectuals a new opportunity. They capitalized on the spirit of change that swept through Western society during the tumultuous Sixties and applied this spirit to the Council, which falsely and dishonestly became their catalyst for the reformation of Catholic church architecture. No longer were they limited to constructing new modernist churches; they quickly found that they could now invoke the Council to advocate the structural reform of existing churches. It made selling their renovation and remodeling ideas much easier.

The renovations that immediately followed the Council were arguably the most drastic. Altars, statues, shrines, communion rails, confessionals, and kneelers were removed from many churches. Others were whitewashed — murals and frescoes succumbed to the roller. "Disregarding the warnings and legislation of the Holy See, many people [made] unwarranted changes in places of worship under the pretext of carrying out the reform of the liturgy and thus [...] caused the disfigurement or loss of priceless works of art."[2]

Despite the Vatican warning issued to the world's bishops in the 1971 document *Opera Artis*[3] church renovators steam-rolled ahead. The archi-liturgical theories of the Sixties were eventually embodied into a document called "Environment and Art in Catholic Worship," released by the U.S. Bishops' Committee on the Liturgy in 1978. This

---

[2] *Opera Artis*, Sacred Congregation of the Clergy, 1971, no. 4.

[3] This Vatican instruction warned bishops that it was their duty to safeguard the patrimony of the Church under their care: "[B]ishops, no matter how hard pressed by their responsibilities, must take seriously the care of places of worship and sacred objects. They bear singular witness to the reverence of the people toward God and deserve such care also because of their historic and artistic value" (*Opera Artis*, no. 4).

document seemed to officially ratify both the theory and practice of the archi-liturgical establishment. Countless churches were literally devastated, a trend which continues unabated today.

As we now understand in retrospect, one of the most contentious issues in Catholic parishes over the past 35 years has been the subject of church renovations. Are renovations necessary? How should they be carried out? What is the ideal for the renovated church? Did Vatican II "require" reform in church architecture? Over and over again these questions provoke quarrels and disputes which too often go unresolved.

For the past three years in my work as editor of *St. Catherine Review* I have spent considerable time reporting on such disputes, showing exactly how "divisive" the proposals for, and results of, church renovations are. Many post-Vatican II renovations, allegedly predicated on the desirability of building "community" in liturgical worship and parish life, have produced the opposite effect: disunity, discord and alienation sometimes leading to an abandonment of the faith.[4]

Proponents of the post-conciliar church renovations would have us believe the Second Vatican Council called for a new paradigm in the design of Catholic churches, one that justifies radical remodeling of existing structures. Although renovation enthusiasts are fond of invoking the Council, when challenged they cannot cite one relevant passage from the Council's documents to support their claims and further, they tend to ignore the clearly articulated recommendations of *Sacrosanctum Concilium*, the

---

[4] "When churches renovate," says Detroit Catholic Ron Stults, a self-employed businessman who has conducted an informal survey of renovated parishes, "you can generally expect to see a 20% drop in weekly giving, and about the same drop in Mass attendance. People either stop going to Mass altogether, or they find a more traditional church" (*The Wanderer*, April 31, 1995).

Council's Constitution on the Sacred Liturgy.[5] The direction these renovations generally take is not one based on Church teaching or even officially approved theological doctrine. Rather, Catholics are being asked to accept the new church designs on the basis of subjective and contrived opinions[6] that are passed off as authoritative mandates of the Church.

The man in the pew instinctively resists the design proposals. But church renovators have learned much in the first two to three decades of their profession's experience with America's Catholic parishes. Today's renovators, those who comprise the archi-liturgical establishment, form an elite few whose *modus operandi* is to effectively "deprogram" and "re-educate" parishioners in their new paradigm through a carefully devised process, one that is less than honest.

Since I first began reporting on church renovation projects I have heard from Catholics all over the country. Almost all describe the same dishonest process and the same architectural results. Others tell of warning signs of an impending project—capital fund drives, for example,

---

[5] One wonders how the same liturgists interpret the exhortation in *Sacrosanctum Concilium* that "the use of the Latin language is to be preserved in the Latin rites," (no. 36.1) or that "the Church acknowledges Gregorian chant as proper to the Roman liturgy: therefore, other things being equal, it should be given pride of place in liturgical services," (no. 116) or that "the practice of placing sacred images in churches so that they may be venerated by the faithful is to be firmly maintained," (no. 124) or that "ordinaries must be very careful to see that sacred furnishings and works of value are not disposed of or allowed to deteriorate" (no. 126).

[6] Such a subjective and contrived opinion is the proposition that there are two different and opposed "presences" of Christ—one "static" in the reserved Blessed Sacrament and the other an "active" presence in the communal celebration of the Eucharist. Many Catholics, including bishops, find this theological opinion to be offensive. Nevertheless countless renovators use this to justify removing the tabernacle from the sanctuary or even the main body of the church.

for "repainting" or "restoration" or "expansion." Many simply say: "This once happened to us!"

In short, there is a blueprint for the renovation process. It has been tried in countless parishes across the continent and too often been ruthlessly implemented over the complaints of confused parishioners.

The first three chapters in this handbook introduce this blueprint by examining a new church professional known as the "liturgical design consultant," his theories, his means, and his methods.

The last three chapters provide parishioners with the necessary knowledge, resources and references to challenge the prevailing fads and opinions in liturgical design and architecture. Through an appeal to the authentic teachings of the Church, past and present, Catholics ought now to be better prepared to diffuse the cliché archi-liturgical rhetoric used against them during the church renovation process.

It is hoped that the present work might give the average lay Catholic a clear understanding of the renovation process and ultimately the knowledge necessary to bring about honesty and integrity in the renovation of existing churches as well as in the construction of new ones.

MICHAEL S. ROSE
Cincinnati, Ohio

CHAPTER 1

The Roots of Today's Renovations
Why Are They Remodeling Our Traditional Churches?

⍟⍟

"IT WOULD HAVE BEEN very helpful for all sorts of parishioners and countless parish committees over the past two decades to know that EACW had no juridically binding or obligatory force," wrote Msgr. William Smith in 1998, twenty years after the release of the document which has become the manifesto of the modernist church renovation movement.[7] Yet only in recent years has the man in the pew come to understand that "Environment and Art in Catholic Worship" is *not* a set of specific directives ratified by the U.S. bishops to be used when churches are renovated.

Notre Dame professor and architect Duncan Stroik describes EACW as "a document of architectural reductionism that reflects a liturgical reductionism. It is fearful of symbols, complexity, history, art and even architecture."[8] EACW, a document of little authority but of massive application, was released in 1978 as a provisional draft statement by the Bishops Committee on Liturgy (BCL) under

---

[7] Smith, Msgr. William Smith, "The Place of a Tabernacle," *Homiletic & Pastoral Review*, December, 1998.

[8] Stroik, Duncan, "Environment and Art in Catholic Worship: A Critique," *Sacred Architecture*, Summer, 1999.

the leadership of San Francisco's then-Archbishop John Quinn.[9] Yet the BCL improperly issued EACW in the name of the National Conference of Catholic Bishops, implying the tacit approval of the Holy See. Canonist Duane L.C.M. Galles outlines the extent of its usage to justify objectionable changes during the renovation process:

> Since 1978 not a few dioceses adopted EACW's recommendations as a set of "directives" to be employed during the renovation of existing churches as well as in the design and construction of new ones. EACW is cited as the authority for the sometimes drastic changes such as destruction of communion rails, ripping out of high altars and replacing them with "tables" in the center of the church building, moving the reserved Blessed Sacrament out of the sanctuary, etc...
>
> The following assertion made by the administrator of a parish in the Archdiocese of Cincinnati is typical: "Many who object to the design do not realize that the Church has given rather specific directives for Catholic worship space. The National Conference of Catholic Bishops has published 'Environment and Art in Catholic Worship.' If major repair work is to be done, this authoritative teaching from the Bishops has to be a guide. Please do not interpret this as an endorsement of the proposed redesign. But the design of worship space is not simply a matter of taste; all must come to terms with the directives from the Bishops.[10]

These church renovators, who once were able to successfully appeal to the alleged authority of EACW, are now finding they are being challenged on that point. Thus, renovators now tend to make a more general appeal to

---

[9] It is "widely held that the text was the work of one person, Fr. Robert Hovda, a well known liturgical consultant who has since passed away" (Ibid.)

[10] Galles, J.C.D., Duane LCM, "EACW: What Force Does It Have?" *Christifidelis*, Sept. 8, 1993.

"post-conciliar documents" to justify their design proposals. It seems to matter little to them whether or not EACW
can legitimately be regarded as a set of authoritative directives; they continue to promote the same design recommendations outlined in the 1978 document. Actually their
recommendations normally go far beyond the EACW
guidelines. This is because their renovation proposals don't
really have their genesis with EACW, but that document
does translate much of the archi-liturgical theory of the
1960's and early 70's into practical guidelines. For that, the
document is significant.

The practical recommendations of today's renovators
as well as those of decades past are clearly based on the
archi-liturgical theories of the 1960's. Protestant architect
Edward A. Sövik was one of the leading theorists and
practitioners of that time. His book, *Architecture in Worship*,
published in 1973, continues to be warmly recommended
to parishes by today's Catholic church renovators. What is
significant about his book—released five years before
EACW—is that it articulates the ideology behind his practical recommendations. He forthrightly discloses his motiva-
tion and his desired results: to continue where the reformation Protestants left off four hundred years ago. If we
can understand Sövik's 1973 archi-liturgical ideology, we
can better understand the impetus driving today's church
renovations and the ramifications of the specific design
recommendations promoted by both Sövik and Catholic
church renovators.

Sövik states his thesis thus:

The history of the church building through the Middle
Ages is a record of a more explicit expression of a theology, a liturgy, and a piety that contradicted in important ways the essential message of Jesus. And when the
Protestant and Catholic reformations of the sixteenth
century came, the architectural forms that resulted were
only partially corrective. The destruction of images and

relics and the rearrangement of furniture in the existing buildings, and the sharp contrasts of form that appeared in some of the few new places of worship built
in those times, did not effectively bring the minds of
churchmen back into harmony with the minds of the
early church.[11]

Sövik correctly states that architecture is a more influential factor in the life of society than most people suppose. "The incompleteness of the Reformation in terms of
architecture was no doubt the result of the longevity of architecture," explains Sövik. He laments the fact that these
medieval edifices are not easily removed or changed. Even
after the iconoclasm of the Reformation, writes Sövik,
"The 'houses of God' from medieval times continued to
stand, continued to assert themselves as 'houses of God'
because of their strong ecclesial character, and continued
to teach the people around them that there ought to be
such a place as a 'house of God.'" [12] He opines that neither
Jesus nor the Fathers of the Church wanted any such edifice and we should work toward the elimination of such a
"misguided medieval pattern." Sövik is further distressed
that most of the churches built within the last 400 years—
both Catholic and Protestant—have continued to establish
"holy places," more or less on the medieval pattern.

To move beyond this medieval pattern, Sövik argues for
the return of what he calls the "non-church," or a "house of
the people," which he defines as a structure which should
not be a church but simply a place through which the people of the church can minister.

He writes: "Down through the centuries church buildings have not been consistently seen as exclusively places of
worship. Church buildings have been multi-purpose

---

[11] Sövik, E.A., *Architecture for Worship*, Minneapolis: Augsburg Publishing
House, 1973, page 18.
[12] Ibid., page 19.

buildings, houses for people, used for a variety of public and secular activities that nourish the human and 'secular' life." [13] Sövik states this as the ideal for liturgical worship space, and he devotes his entire book to providing practical suggestions to accomplish this through architecture.

He believes that in the United States the Puritans and the Methodists once did this well: "The Puritans built meeting houses, quite secular in form and detail, and used them for any public assembly. The early Methodists had their places of worship in any convenient barn or loft, and when they built, their architecture was consciously non-ecclesiastical." [14]

Like the early Methodist's prototype, Sövik's non-church should *not* be divided into a sanctuary and a nave. It should not even be referred to using traditional terms of church architecture, lest there be confusion. "It is a meeting place for people," he writes. "It will be so different a thing from the usual 'church' that any of these terms which carry the sense of special purpose liturgical centers is inappropriate." [15] Sövik proposes instead to use the word "centrum." A centrum, he explains, "is a place for more than one purpose, and must be seen, and so used. If it is not, if for one reason or another it is reserved for the liturgy, it will sooner or later be thought of as the 'house of God'; and then it will be thought of as a holy place; and then other places will be seen as profane or secular." [16]

Sövik says he wants a "throw-away" interior for his centrum. "For the space itself must be simple, allowing for many configurations of use. And the furnishings and symbolic devices will be portable, so they may be varied, re-

---

[13] Ibid., page 19.
[14] Ibid., page 21.
[15] Ibid., page 68.
[16] Ibid., page 70.

placed, augmented or abandoned as the parishioners of future times desire."[17]

How then should one properly design the throw-away interior of a centrum which will not be mistaken by anyone to be a "holy place" or a "house of God"? Sövik proposes the following:

- Remove the pews and replace them with portable chairs;

- Set up a separate room to reserve the eucharistic species (if necessary at all);

- Remove any artwork which might be construed as strictly religious in content, e.g., religious statues or icons;

- Eliminate the traditional sanctuary by bringing the "table" into the congregation and arranging the chairs around the table;

- Eliminate the use of crucifixes and Latin crosses in favor of portable Greek crosses ("plus signs") which would be used only in processions and during the liturgy.

Many Catholics will recognize Sövik's proposal as the same basic scheme which has been used repeatedly in the renovation of their churches since the early 1970's; it is the same practical advice which is offered in the BCL's *Environment & Art in Catholic Worship*. He did not in fact intend his book only for his Protestant co-religionists, but marketed it as a handbook for *both* Catholic and Protestant congregations: "[E]specially useful for church leaders, clergy, and building committees of Protestant and Roman Catholic churches, it offers practical, economical advice on

---

[17] Ibid., page 71.

both the remodeling of existing structures and the construction of new ones."[18]

The theory upon which Sövik's proposal is predicated is both interesting and revealing. He begins by making some observations on what he considers to be "good liturgical space": It should be one space, he suggests; its horizontal proportions should not be too elongated so as not to give the impression of a traditional church arrangement, which he sees as problematic. "The design tradition we have inherited from the Renaissance," he writes, "has led us to assume that every large room should be organized symmetrically, and we tend to look for some dominating feature about which the room comes to focus. If we declare that *people* are really the focus of what happens in the liturgy then any very strong architectural focus can subvert our intentions."[19] Accordingly Sövik argues against the tabernacle, crucifix, cross or altar, each of which tends to become a central focal point in liturgical space.

Instead of using Renaissance or medieval church plans as precedents for the design of his non-church centrum, Sövik proposes that designers look for prototypes to the Japanese tea house and the dining room/living room combos which became popular in post-World War II houses. His practical recommendations are consistent with these prototypes:

On the issue of **pews or chairs**, Sövik writes: "Nothing gives the conventional church building its ecclesiastical character more than do pews and nothing inhibits flexibility more than pews. Chairs have the advantages of flexibility."[20] Out with the pews then, he recommends, and in with portable chairs. Sövik does not want anyone to mistake his centrum for a church.

---

[18] Ibid., back cover.
[19] Ibid., page 76.
[20] Ibid., page 77.

EACW in a similar fashion recommends: "When multi-function use of the space is indicated by the needs of either the faith community or of the surrounding city, town, or rural area which the faith community services, a certain flexibility or movability should be considered even for the essential furnishings" (no. 65). Since pews offer neither flexibility nor movability the church renovator argues that portable chairs are ideal. Even when multi-function use of the space is not indicated, the renovator will still often advocate the chair over the pew—it is the fashion of the day.

On the topic of elimination of **the sanctuary**, Sövik writes: "It should be recognized that the intent of a dais or platform is not to accent a sanctuary as separate from the congregation space. It is simply to provide enough elevation so that certain liturgical functions which need visibility can get it."[21]

EACW addresses the topic in a more nuanced manner, yet arrives at the same end result: "Special attention must be given to the *unity of the entire liturgical space*. Before considering the distinction of roles within the liturgy, the space should communicate integrity (a sense of oneness, of wholeness) and a sense of being the gathering place of the initiated community" (no. 53).

Writing about the "**eucharistic table**" Sövik states, "The eucharistic table is usually called an altar, but ought to be distinguished from the sacrificial altars of other religions. Its genus is the dining room table. It is the table at which the ritual meal is served, and its symbolic value is like that of the dining table in the home. The eucharistic table ought to be located where it can be sensed as belonging to the whole gathered community."[22]

In its section on the altar, EACW recommends that the "holy *table*" be designed for the "action of the community." It should therefore "not be elongated, but square or

---

[21] Ibid., page 81.
[22] Ibid., page 83.

slightly rectangular... [and] central in any eucharistic celebration" (no 72). Liturgical design consultants are fond of interpreting this section of EACW as a ringing endorsement of throwing the altar "into the midst of the people." The important sacrificial aspect of the Mass seems to have been dismissed.

Sövik also argues for the **elimination of kneeling** to receive communion because, he claims, "a celebration ought to be joyful, but kneeling is not the posture of joy; in a communion one ought to be particularly conscious of the community; ... but kneeling is not a posture in which we can properly commune."[23]

EACW offers no advice on accommodating the traditional posture of kneeling during the liturgy; it only exhorts designers to strive for "a seating pattern and furniture that do not constrict people, but encourage them to move about when it is appropriate" (no. 68). Although one wonders how often it is "appropriate" to move about during the Mass, the church renovator interprets that exhortation as justification for seating without kneelers, since kneelers tend to "constrict" people.[24]

On the issue of **visual projections**, Sövik argues that in new buildings and remodeled churches, technology for visual projection and moving pictures must be accommodated. "If a church can provide a good place for cinema, it has an additional way of serving a community and making a building more useful."[25]

Five years later EACW makes the same recommendation in paragraph 104: "It is safe to say that a new church

---

[23] Ibid., page 87.

[24] Prominent church renovator Father Richard Vosko is fond of saying, "When we get to the pearly gates, God isn't going to ask us whether we had kneelers, but God will ask us if we fed the hungry." (Gintoff, Ethel M., "Cathedral renovation: Enhance liturgy, don't destroy, says design consultant," *Catholic Herald,* June 24, 1999, page 1.)

[25] Sövik, E.A., *Architecture for Worship,* Minneapolis: Augsburg Publishing House, 1973, page 91.

building or renovation project should make provision for screens and/or walls which will make the projection of films, slides and filmstrips visible to the entire assembly."[26]

Sövik also demands that never are recognizable **crucifixes** to be used. He writes: "The iconoclastic reformers removed the corpus and left the Protestants with a symbol which is the image of an instrument of torture. We have become used to this curiosity so that we most often forget what it is, or suppose the absence of a corpus is an adequate symbol for resurrection. Would an electric chair symbolize resurrection? Or would we accept the electric chair as a proper symbol of the Christian faith if Jesus had been executed in this century?"[27] Thus, Sövik recommends neither the crucifix nor the traditional Latin cross be used. He argues for use of the so-called "Greek cross" which appears in the shape of a (+) "plus-sign." He believes that this form is obscure enough not to be identified with the sacrificial cross, the "instrument of torture." Sövik, also opposed to large crosses, argues for a single, "small" processional cross ("one doesn't need to suppose that there must be a gigantic symbol somewhere, as if making a cross big demonstrates superior piety," he writes), one that is "among the people" during the liturgy, and whisked away at its completion.

So too EACW recommends, instead of a large fixed cross or crucifix, "a processional cross with a floor standard, in contrast to one that is permanently hung or affixed to a wall" (no. 88). And although the Greek cross is not specifically called for by EACW, the church renovator consistently advocates the use of the "plus-sign-shaped cross."

---

[26] Bishops Committee on Liturgy, "Environment and Art in Catholic Worship," 1978, paragraph 104.
[27] Sövik, E.A., *Architecture for Worship*, Minneapolis: Augsburg Publishing House, 1973, page 109.

Sövik concludes his treatise by illustrating his ideal of the non-church centrum renovation. He cites the work of St. Katherine's parish in Baltimore, Maryland (remember, this is back in 1973):

> Here Fr. Joseph Connolly, a priest whose sense of liturgy and human concern belong together, is leading the parish to immerse themselves in providing for the welfare of the people in the area. He now calls his church building a 'community service center.' The nave has been cleared of pews and other hindrances. It has become the meeting place for any kind of assembly that needs a place, and movable screens can separate different kinds of activities that occur simultaneously. Children swarm. Rock music, dances, clinics, educational enterprises, eating and drinking, even a homosexual group have been given shelter. For if Jesus didn't reject the company of publicans and prostitutes, why should the church be less hospitable?[28]

Catholic church renovators have obviously been inspired or affected by Protestant architect Edward Sövik for the past three decades at least. He has enjoyed guru status among the archi-liturgical establishment, his architectural work is held up as exemplary, and he is regarded by many church renovators as a mentor. Indeed, his archi-liturgical ideology of secularizing the sacred was *en vogue* among liturgists during the mid-1970's as it is today. Sövik and kindred spirits were caught up with the liturgical experimentation of the late 1960's and early '70's. Their penultimate goal was the elimination of the sacred from church architecture, their ultimate goal the elimination of the church building.

EACW does not admit that these are its goals. Nevertheless, "it seems that the BCL produced a document worthy of the 'non church' promoted by Protestant architect

---

[28] Ibid., pp. 118-19

[Edward] Sövik."[29] Indeed, the practical recommendations offered by Sövik in 1973 to create his ideal throw-away, non-church centrum are the same recommendations offered by the Bishops' Committee on Liturgy in their controversial 1978 document. Further, liturgical design consultants tend to interpret many of the passages in EACW to justify their own archi-liturgical proclivities, so much so that one wonders if it is the Sövik manifesto to which they look for inspiration rather than the BCL's document, as controversial as it may be on its own.

---

[29] Stroik, Duncan, "Environment and Art in Catholic Worship: A Critique," *Sacred Architecture*, Summer, 1999.

CHAPTER 2

The Liturgical Design Consultant
The Professional Church Renovator & His Techniques

ഌരൂ

W E ARE EXPERIENCING a crisis of fashion: If we were to review the past 35 years of church renovation projects we would quickly come to understand that the specific design work of the church renovator is not mandated by the Church (as he will invariably claim), but driven by fads that are subject to the ever-changing archi-liturgical fashion. The renovation designs undertaken in the 1970's, for instance, are so dated that they are an embarrassment to church renovators of the 1990's. The fads promoted by the current archi-liturgical establishment are limited only by the caprice of the arbiter of architectural fashion, the renovation theorist.[30]

---

[30] An obvious example of archi-liturgical fashion is the placement of the baptismal font. Renovators of the 90's now readily admit that their recommendations in the 1970's, to locate the font "up front" in the sanctuary, was not the best solution. Liturgical design consultant Christine Reinhard of Harbor Springs, Michigan writes in her educational handout on "The Baptistery" that "Like many things since Vatican II, the baptistery is still evolving" in shape, size and location. "In its evolution since Vatican II, the font has been all over the church. Being able to see the font during the baptism was first thought to be the critical issue. Now a consensus is starting to form that visibility, while important is a

It may be helpful to understand that our times are not the only that have been beset with problems of church fashion. In his classic novel of 1831, *The Hunchback of Notre Dame*, Victor Hugo explains that his beloved Cathedral of Notre Dame de Paris was once the subject of a "barbaric" renovation. Hugo beautifully expressed his sorrow and indignation at the "numberless degradations and mutilations" which the hand of man had inflicted upon the venerable monument.

"Upon the face of this old queen of the French cathedrals beside each wrinkle we constantly find a scar," wrote Hugo. "*Tempus edax, homo edacior.* Which we would willingly render thus: Time is blind, but man is stupid."

Historians often blame the French Revolution as occasioning the severe disrepair that necessitated the restoration project undertaken by Eugene Emmanuel Violet-le-Duc in the 1850's. Yet Hugo criticized what Parisians of the 18th century had done to the great cathedral in the name of fashion rather than revolution.[31] He drew up a list of his

---

secondary issue... You may have already guessed that the location of choice is becoming the entrance of the worship space... Initially, when fonts were placed at the entrance, they were in the gathering space, or narthex. This has two drawbacks. The first drawback is that it really breaks up the flow of ritual when the entire body must move through doors to another space. Secondly, the gathering space is the place for random gathering, an important social experience. The nave, or main body of the church, is the place for ritual gathering, for the sacraments. When the font is placed up front, it says, 'Look but don't touch.' Only the priest goes up there. We don't want to enshrine the font like another tabernacle."

[31] Hugo wrote: "But who has thrown down the two ranges of statues? Who has left the niches empty? Who has cut in the middle of the central portal that new and bastard pointed arch? Who has dared to hang in it that heavy unmeaning wooden gate, carved a la Louis XV, besides the arabesques of Biscornette? The men, the architects, the artists of our times. And—if we enter the interior of the edifice—who has overturned that colossal St. Christopher, proverbial for his magnitude among statues, as the Grand' Salle of the Palais was among halls, as the spire of Strasburg among steeples? And those myriads of statues which thronged

criticisms: the colored stained-glass windows had been removed, the interior was white-washed, the tower over the
central part of the cathedral had been ripped off, the
shape of the central entrance to the Cathedral had been
deformed, and the chapels were filled with ugly decora-
tions. He explains that the ruin of his beloved Notre Dame
was precipitated by three forces:

1. Time, which "has gradually made deficiencies here
and there, and has gnawed over its whole surface";

2. "Violence, brutalities, contusions, fractures—these
are the works of revolutions." This is the type of destruction, wrote Hugo, wrought by indiscriminate
revolutionary violence; and

3. Fashion, which, Hugo contested, has done more
mischief than revolutions: "It has cut to the quick—it
has attacked the very bone and framework of the art."

Hugo observed that time and revolution devastated the
edifice "with impartiality and grandeur." Yet fashion was

---

all the intercolumniations of the nave and the choir—kneeling, standing, equestrian—men, women, children—kings, bishops, warriors—in
stone, in marble, in gold, in silver, in brass, and even in wax—who has
brutally swept them out? It is not Time that has done it.

"And who has substituted for the old Gothic altar, splendidly
loaded with shrines and reliquaries, that heavy sarcophagus of marble,
with angels' heads and clouds, which looks like an unmatched specimen
from the Val-de-Grâce or the Invalides! Who has stupidly fixed that
heavy anachronism of stone into the Carlovingian pavement of Hercan-
dus? Was it not Louis XIV fulfilling the vow of Louis XIII? And who has
put cold white glass in place of those deep-tinctured panes which made
the wondering eyes of our forefathers hesitate between the round window over the grand doorway and the pointed ones of the chancel? And
what would a subchanter of the sixteenth century say could he see that
fine yellow-washing with which the Vandal archbishops have besmeared
their cathedral?"

perpetrated by "school-trained architects, licensed, privileged, and patented, degrading with all the discernment and selection of bad taste." Thus, Hugo is saying that the worst destruction was perpetrated not by the atheistic iconoclasts of the bloody French Revolution, as many historians would have it, but by these school-trained architects, slaves to bad taste.

Hugo accused these men who assume the character of the architect of willful destruction, perversion, and recreation, all in the name of fashion. The results? Mutilations, amputations, dislocation of members—"renovations."

Today, to appease liturgical fashion, another caste of "school-trained architects," licensed, privileged and patented by a local bishop, move from one house of worship to the next, requiring the disfigurement of priceless works of sacred art, in the end mangling the entire edifice of the church—in its form as well as in its meaning, in its consistency as well as in its beauty.

Today's school-trained architect, however, is usually no architect. Rather, he appears in the character of a new church professional known as the "liturgical design consultant."[32] Judging from the similarities in the techniques used by most consultants, one can only conclude that there is but one simple font for the promotion of the archiliturgical agenda.

According to Franciscan Sister Sandra Schweitzer of Indianapolis, in 1999 there were only 103 "certified" liturgical design consultants in the United States. Design consultants are certified by an accrediting body by the name of the Association of Consultants for Liturgical Space (ACLS). Sister Schweitzer, an entrepreneur design consultant her-

---

[32] There are variations to this title, such as "environment and art consultant," "liturgical consultant," etc. Father Richard S. Vosko, for instance, bills himself as a "designer and consultant for worship environments."

self, is among the elite 103. [33] Most of those certified in the field of liturgical design are trained in a three-year program at the Catholic Theological Union in Chicago,[34] known for its accommodation of rank dissenters and promoters of the reform-Church movement. These certified design consultants along with certain liturgists, who are much more numerous, comprise the archi-liturgical establishment in the Church.

While appearing to give architectural advice, the design consultant's real function is to manipulate parishioners into accepting controversial changes to their church building and into believing that their own input — their ideas of what a parish church building should be — is being taken into consideration in the renovation of their church. To this end, diocesan liturgical committees recommend these facilitators[35] to engineer the whole process that a parish must undergo to achieve a preordained design with little or no resistance from parishioners.

---

[33] Schoettle, Anthony, "Nun of her business: Sister sheds traditional role to begin consulting firm," *Indianapolis Business Journal*, March 8-14, 1999, page 1.

[34] Ibid.

[35] Mrs. Karen Kane, associate director of the Archdiocese of Cincinnati's Office of Worship attended a meeting of the Growth [i.e., Renovation] Steering Committee at St. Philip Church in Morrow, Oh. A week later she presented the Committee with formal recommendations from her office. Kane's recommendations to the Committee, according to the Committee's minutes from their July, 1997 meeting include "that we inform parishioners as to 'why' changes are necessary in their worship area so that approval of the Archdiocese Environment and Art Committee can be obtained and that we use liturgical consultants in the design of the worship space to facilitate this approval... Without a solid foundation of formation the assembly will not be able to understand 'why' the tabernacle is not in the main body of the church, or 'why' the assembly is facing one another, or 'why' the baptismal font takes on such a prominent role in the space. They will simply feel that these are the new laws by which they must abide, rather than their faith helping them to understand the law" [sic].

The archi-liturgical establishment has long realized that the process is as important as the design program. Instead of simply telling a congregation that their tabernacle will be removed from the main body of the church, that the seating will be rearranged, that statues, shrines, crucifixes and stations of the cross will be relegated to the diocesan museum or the antique shop, etc. (as was the tactic of the 1970's), the design consultant is introduced to facilitate a process that forges an impression that the parish contributed, or at least had the opportunity to contribute, to the design of their remodeled church.

The Delphi Technique

This manipulative strategy is popularly identified as the "Delphi Technique." First developed by the Rand Corporation in the 1950's, and later applied for purposes of psychological warfare, it is an effective method of gaining acceptance of a controversial proposal, whether it is the Goals 2000-education model, the environmental agenda, or the new archi-liturgical paradigm. In group-settings this technique is an unethical method of achieving "consensus."[36] It requires well-trained professionals known as "facilitators" ('change agents'), who "deliberately escalate tension among group members, pitting one faction against another to make a certain preordained viewpoint appear obvious and sensible, while making opposing views appear ridiculous."[37]

In her book *Educating for the New World Order,* educator Beverly Eakman explains that those in positions of

---

[36] "Consensus" is a term used by facilitators using methods such as the Delphi Technique. Their definition of consensus is not an orthodox one. Their usage does not mean agreement by all involved, but rather indicates that a majority of those involved are no longer willing to object.

[37] Stuter, Lynn. "Focus: Using the Delphi Technique to Achieve Consensus," *Education Reporter,* November, 1998.

authority and power are concerned with giving the illusion that there is "community participation in decision-making processes, while in fact lay citizens are being squeezed out."[38]

Not suspecting that such a technique exists, most people unwittingly participate in this manipulative stratagem. In doing so they become part of what is known as a "consensus circle." The Russian term for consensus circle is "soviet." Once the "soviet" is established, the community—a parish, for instance—necessarily becomes accountable for the "decisions" that are made, since the input of the people has supposedly been taken into consideration. Facilitators speak of this process as "achieving consensus."[39]

The process is important because parishioners must believe their input is integral to the result if they are to financially support the project. To persuade them of this the design consultant is the key. He is the change agent

---

[38] A few years ago, for instance, the city of Spokane, Washington hired a "facilitator" for $47,000 to guide the direction of city government. A group of disenfranchised citizens were brought together to "discuss" what they felt needed to be changed at the local government level. A compilation of the results of these "discussions" allegedly influenced the writing of Spokane's city charter. In reality, however, the facilitator was hired merely to give the citizens the illusion that their input influenced the writing of the charter. The $47,000 facilitator led the citizens through a process to make them assume ownership of a predetermined outcome.

[39] In the Spring, 1999 "Restoration, Renovation & Renewal Project Update" newsletter published by St. Francis Xavier Church in Petoskey, Michigan, the editor describes the "consensus model of decision making." He writes: "The Renovation, Restoration & Renewal Committee is operating under a model called consensus. This means the group never votes on anything... We operate this way because we have been directed to by Vatican II. The American Council of Bishops [sic] encourages it, and most dioceses actively direct all groups operating within their churches to function in this fashion... If the opinion is divided, then we discuss further until consensus is reached. A consensus does not mean that everyone agrees with the decision. It means that while some may not personally like it, they can see why for some good reason it should be done, and they accept the decision."

who will lead the parish to reach the preset outcome—the new archi-liturgical paradigm. His only purpose is to lead the people to accept radical and disturbing changes to their church building and their devotional life. These changes are disturbing precisely because the people sense, even without being able to articulate it, that these changes will affect their interior spiritual disposition.

One feature of the Delphi Technique, commonly used today in academic and corporate settings, is for the facilitator to give the impression he knows everything on the topic at hand and that his audience is made up of ignorant do-gooders at best. When an organization wants to introduce a new paradigm to its employees, it will enlist an outside "authority" who is introduced as an "expert" in the field. This person functions as the facilitator. Without him, the task of removing the old paradigm is not easily accomplished. Removing attachment to the old model is essential to the process.

Many public school systems, for instance, are actively and aggressively replacing traditional teaching methods with a new paradigm known as "outcome-based education." To accomplish this task, every last teacher in that school system must be "freed" from the old methods they use before they will readily accept the new agenda, method, or paradigm. A facilitator is invited from some renowned "Teachers' College" in order to ridicule these teachers' beliefs and practices and to make them doubt the way they have been approaching the teaching of their subject matter, sometimes for decades.

Once doubt is instilled in their minds, the facilitator paves the way for the new paradigm. Those who resist are singled out for harsh treatment by the facilitator, who is trained to manipulate the docile of the flock to turn against the "dissenters." Peer pressure is applied until the dissenters either change their long-held opinions and attachments or until they leave. That is when "consensus" is reached.

The same methods are employed with regard to church renovations and the construction of new churches. The design consultant is invited into a parish community to undermine the devotions, methods and faith of its people.[40] The facilitator will necessarily come from outside the parish community, often from another diocese. He treats those who oppose the renovation as "liturgical retards" and "spiritual midgets," ridiculing their "pre-Vatican II form of worship."

The ultimate purpose of effecting a paradigm shift in Catholic church architecture is to radically remake Catholicism by striking at the outward manifestations of the Catholic faith. The old paradigm of nearly 1500 years is one of "familiarity" and "mystery," a holy building set in a

---

[40] To illustrate here are two quotes from consultant Fr. Richard S. Vosko as he addresses St. Theresa Church in Succasunna, New Jersey in 1982: "I don't mean to be offensive at this moment but I think it may be opportune for me to say here and now that in our Church there are a lot of people who absolutely agree with everything the Church teaches. You know people like that? Are you a person like that—who never questions anything that the Church teaches? My mother's like that. My father's like that. I think my sister is like that and I got to admit that when I go to bed at night I'm a little like that... But there are a lot of people who are just rely on blind faith and trust and accept everything the Church teaches without ever thinking about it. Can you identify with that? Morality issues? Fish on Friday issues? How many of you had meat tonight? Not too many, I bet. Good, old time Catholics when you come down to it. Friday is for fish." On the subject of Eucharistic devotion, Fr. Vosko told his Succasunna audience: "One reason why our churches are so susceptible to crime is because they are empty during the week. Maybe people who have organized vigils before the Sacrament—that's a wonderful practice to keep vigil, to take turns keeping vigil over the Blessed Sacrament, that is primarily saved to take to the sick and dying—that is what the Church teaches us. And I think it's a wonderful practice to take turns keeping watch just in case. Well, just think if your mother and father needed Holy Communion on their death bed. Wouldn't it be nice to know you can go to that tabernacle and find the Body of Christ in it?"

place that gave the community a sense of continuity and security:

> The architectural style and furnishings in the [American] neighborhood churches were similar in many ways to those in European homelands. The quiet ambience, the ubiquitous smell of incense, the flicker of candles dancing in the darkness, the almost eerie presence of innumerable images, laser-like beams streaming through stained glass windows, immense high altars, and the surreptitious presentation of the Mass contributed to the familiar and mysterious milieu. My boyhood church was the church of immigrants clinging to the past for continuity and identity. It sustained what people believed to be expressions of mystery. It was where God dwelled.[41]

In contrast, the new paradigm reflects the ideology and practical recommendations of Edward Sövik's parish centrum. Fr. Vosko echoes Sövik when he describes his ideal "church of tomorrow" as one that is primarily secular: "similar to the other familiar public spaces, buildings that are well designed and constructed to accommodate large numbers of people in comfortable and pleasant ways."[42] He writes hopefully that it:

- will tell the "faith stories" of this age;
- will be mysterious not because of any architectural or artistic sleight of hand but because of the respectful and gracious way people conduct themselves;
- will become, once again, a house for the church (rather than a "house of God");

---

[41] Vosko, Fr. Richard S., "The future space of worship spaces: in between no more and not yet," *The Catholic World*, March-April, 1994.
[42] Ibid.

- will use "sophisticated building materials and technologies," not the natural and more expensive materials used in the churches of the past;
- will be "ecologically sound" and "completely energy efficient";
- will reflect and symbolize "the gospel message of care and respect for people and the environment";
- will focus on the assembly "gathered about the font and table";
- will stimulate the senses through the incorporation of mobile art, holography, and computerized projections;
- will incorporate natural scents to "trigger the full sensual capacity of the community causing interactive, conscious and subliminal participation in the celebration of word and sacrament";
- will more fully integrate music, singing, drama and body movement into the worship action;
- will include "other sectors" devoted to bible study, prayer sessions, counseling and support groups;
- will have a database of biographies so that the community may be able "to interact with holographic images of religious folk heroes";
- will feature sculptures, weavings and paintings of "saintly personalities" in its "inner and outer gardens and pathways";
- will house the "eucharistic bread" in "its own chapel sector."[43]

Anatomy of the process

The renovation process follows a typical course that can be broken down into certain set phases. Most consultants will use the approach described in some form. However,

---

[43] Ibid.

the phases may occur in a different order, may be simplified, or modified. One ought to bear in mind that the process here set forth depends on parishioner ignorance and apathy to succeed as fully as possibly. In most cases, the more ignorance and apathy among parishioners, the more radical the renovation of their church will be. The process is also designed to wear out opponents of the proposed changes.

Rarely is a renovation plan juggernaut completely halted, but it does happen.[44] In other cases, parishioners who were organized and educated were able to bring about significant compromises in the overall renovation plan. If enough parishioners recognize this process *at its beginning*, they will have a better chance at halting the process in its infant stages, before the parish becomes divided.

Phase 1 –A design consultant is hired

The process begins when the decision is made to renovate or build a new church. This may be a long, drawn out process to begin with, to give the parish the impression that the pastoral council or a certain sub-committee of the parish bureaucracy has determined "through careful study and analysis" that the church needs to expand,[45] needs new

---

[44] "On Saturday, March 13... Msgr. John Newstead informed parishioners that, after consultation with Bishop Anthony Tonnos of Hamilton, [Father] Vosko's plan to remove the intricately carved stone reredos with its golden domed tabernacle surmounted by a stone statue of the Virgin Mary, the altar rail, and confessionals—among other proposals—would not go forward because of overwhelming opposition by parishioners.

[45] The idea to radically remodel St. Philip Church in Morrow, Ohio, developed from problems that required attention at the rectory. Since the pastor complained of a lack of privacy and a leaky roof and basement, St. Philip's formed a "Parish Rectory Repair Committee" which later became known as the "Growth Steering Committee." In a January, 1996 Committee meeting the pastor suggested that the parish convert the present rectory into parish offices and buy a new suburban tract

fixtures, desperately needs painting or cleaning, requires handicap access, etc. — some reason to facilitate a renovation project. In other cases the preordained renovation plans are undertaken in conjunction with another parish building project, e.g., expansion of the school building or construction of a new gym or parish center.

The pastor then appoints a steering committee (sometimes called a "core committee") to see the renovation process to its completion. The members of this committee are characterized by their loyalty to the pastor, rather than to their faith or the Church. The pastor counts on the members of this committee to act as apologists for the project. The committee will be informed that a design consultant must be hired. [46] A contract is eventually signed with a consultant, often at the recommendation of diocesan liturgists or the bishop. The consultant's initial objective is to lead the parish to the conclusion that their church is unsuitable for the celebration of the liturgy according to the alleged mandates of Vatican II. Most parishioners at this

---

house for the pastor in the developing subdivision across the street from St. Philip's 42-acre campus. From there an alternative idea developed that the rectory could be converted solely into the pastor's residence and an addition to the church would provide additional office space. In May of 1996 that idea was adopted. Claiming a "probable need" for additional seats in the church in the next ten years (judging from the projected growth of the area), the Growth Steering Committee's expansion proposal grew to include provision for additional "worship space." Thus, a consultant was hired to explain that the whole church must be remodeled if they want to expand.

[46] The fees commanded by the certified design consultant are exorbitant. Well-known consultant Fr. Richard Vosko charges an initial fee of at least $15,000. This fee is typically paid out of parish funds for the work he does in the "preliminary stage." At St. Jude's Church in Detroit, Father Vosko was hired "for $25,000 to convince parishioners of the need to fund a $3.5 million grandiose master plan to make the church more 'hospitable'" (*The Wanderer*, Oct. 31, 1996). The same consultant was hired by Msgr. John Newstead at an initial $60,000 to lead the process to renovate the Church of Our Lady of the Immaculate in Guelph, Ontario (*The Wanderer*, April 1, 1999).

early stage are entirely unaware of the impending renovation project.

Phase 2 –"Restoration" introduced

Articles begin to appear in the parish bulletin or newsletter introducing the idea of "restoration"[47] (rather than "renovation"). The parish will hear sound bite-like distortions of the truth, such as "the church will be restored in a way that reflects its original beauty,"[48] or "the historic and architectural integrity of the church will be respected."[49] This begins the conditioning process to ma-

---

[47] According to Steven Seebohm of Seebohm, Ltd, a company that specializes in historic renovation, "Restoration is the pursuit of maintaining an original historic structure, preventing further damage or deterioration, and/or returning a structure to its original state" (The Parishioner, March 22, 1999).

[48] In the Spring of 1997 the pastor of St. Martin of Tours, Church in Cheviot, Ohio, presented his "Restoration Master Plan" to parishioners. This plan was to "restore the interior of the church to its past splendor" by undertaking the following: "Correcting the water damage by plastering and painting the church; replacing the floor below the church pews; and refinishing the church pews and woodwork." The pastor's plan was published in a fundraising booklet. Based on the information provided in this booklet, many parishioners made generous pledges to effect what they thought would be a noble restoration of their beautiful neo-Romanesque church. The actual project undertaken a year and a half later was not the project for which St. Martin parishioners pledged their money. The renovation actually entailed removal of the tabernacle from the high altar to a separate alcove; demolition of the communion rail and two of the four confessionals, rearrangement of pews, building the sanctuary out into the midst of the assembly, and the addition of a baptism pool at the entrance to the nave.

[49] Commenting on the renovation of Seattle's St. James Cathedral, Catherine Ross of Bellevue, Washington commented, "They said they were going to reclaim the historical integrity of the church, but they wrecked the design scheme. They don't have an Italian Renaissance church anymore. Our cathedral looks like a Reformation-era Catholic church taken over by Protestants who didn't want any 'popish artifacts.'" At the beginning of the process St. James' pastor said he would not "predict in any detail just what specific changes will be made," but as-

nipulate parishioners into accepting major changes to the church. At this point the majority of parishioners are not aware of what is really involved in the project. In many cases this majority believes that new carpet or flooring will be installed, pews repaired, windows cleaned, paintings or statues repaired where necessary. Most will be delighted that these long-needed repairs will soon be addressed. In more recent projects parishioners have been "lured" into supporting the project in its infant stages. They may be told their white-washed statues will be repainted in the original colors, or that the kneelers that were removed during a previous decade will be re-installed. Publicity will be focused on these non-controversial aspects of the renovation, before the other proposals are subtly introduced.

Phase 3 –Educational sessions

The consultant arrives at the parish to begin a series of educational sessions, sometimes billed as a "renewal program." During these sessions the consultant first offers a slide-show lecture of the development of Catholic church architecture from a modernist's viewpoint. The purpose of the slide lecture is to disparage traditionally arranged spaces and to challenge parishioners' notions of what a church should look like—inside and out. It will be interlarded with subjective and contrived theological opinions.

The emphasis during this first session is on the liturgical practices of the first Christian centuries. The message conveyed is this: the early Church's practices were authen-

---

sured all that the "beauty and integrity of an old and venerable structure" would be respected. The cathedral handouts also stated that the 1994 renovation would not "destroy the true architectural beauty of the church" (*The Wanderer*, May 25, 1995).

tic expressions of what Jesus expected of his disciples.[50] Thereafter, as certain liturgical practices developed, the entire Church fell into deep error,[51] an error that was only corrected recently via the Second Vatican Council. The purpose here is to undermine the traditional faith of average pew Catholics, while subtly introducing the preordained plan for their church's archi-liturgical future.

The following sessions will usually be geared toward discussing the history and development of specific design elements, e.g., the tabernacle, the altar, the baptistery, the assembly, the pulpit (or ambo), etc. During these sessions the design consultant explains why the Church "requires" moving the tabernacle out of the sanctuary into a side chapel, why chairs must be used instead of pews, why the church needs to be built "in the round," why there will be no crucifix and why the cross—which will look like a "plus sign"—will only be brought in during the Mass, why there will be no traditional statues, why the existing statue of the Blessed Virgin should be kept in a closet and only brought out on special occasions, etc.

---

[50] "If we go back to the way Jesus did things we'd all be having Mass at our dining room tables with the head of the household leading the prayers. That's the way it was done until things got organized" (Fr. Richard Vosko, Slide show lecture to St. Theresa Church, Succasunna, NJ, 1982).

[51] "[During the Middle Ages] we find all kinds of evidences that priests would insert abuses. They would be elevating the Host several times during liturgy and actually that's where we find [the abuses]. We find that when a priest doesn't quite understand exactly what the proper gesture is, we see there's some kind of elevation of the bread and wine at the preparation rite. Well, there should not be! There's a showing of the bread during the words of institution—that's appropriate. There's a showing of the bread during the doxology at the end of the Eucharistic prayer. There's a showing of the bread at the beginning of the Communion rite. All of these are a holdover from the multiple showings of bread there in the Middle Ages when people would be crying out, according to some of our history books, 'Lift higher, Sir George, lift higher. Hold it up there longer'" (Ibid.).

Here the consultant introduces a new vocabulary to the parish in order to circumvent the traditional concepts associated with certain words. For example, the term "worship space" is used in place of "church." As Sövik explains in his treatise: the word "church" is far too traditional sounding and cannot be used because many Catholics have a preconceived notion of what a "church" should look like, i.e., the old paradigm. Another popular word-change is substituting "table" for "altar" and "presider" for "priest." Consultants want Catholics to forget that a priest is one who offers sacrifice and that an altar is a place on which sacrifice is offered. Likewise, an adoration chapel may be called an "exposition chapel." Adoration of the Blessed Sacrament is considered passé or worse amongst the archi-liturgical establishment.

This phase is characterized by deliberate misinterpretation of Vatican II and an appeal to the "authority" of EACW. The pastor and the consultant will continue to consider the project a "restoration," even though it has become obvious that the consultant is proposing radical changes.

Some parishioners will now begin to object to the false claims made by the consultant. The consultant responds by setting one parishioner's opinion against another's, making those who object to his ideas appear ridiculous, ignorant, inarticulate and rigid. If and when it becomes difficult for the consultant to adequately respond to parishioners' objections, he or the pastor may declare that "No decisions have been made!"[52] The implication here is that if no decisions have been made, there can be no objections.

---

[52] "Commonly heard saying: If someone expresses concern about the changes being promoted the reply may likely be: 'Don't get excited, no decisions have been made yet.' There are two reasons not to accept this answer. First, the paid consultant has repeatedly stated that there are three absolutes. 1) Handicap access to every place in the church; 2) Moving the tabernacle to its own separate space; 3) Installing an adult-sized baptistery. If it looks like a decision, sounds like a decision and

Apart from the educational sessions, the parish begins to hear that "Change is difficult; change involves conversion; conversion is the Church's business; the parish needs to be converted from exaggerated individualism and private devotion to focus on the assembly and community." Both the pastor and his associates often find it useful to deliver homilies on "authority," and "obedience" when dealing with a conservative parish, often dishonestly invoking the Council, the bishops, even Pope John Paul II, to single out the renovation dissenters as "knee-jerk reactionaries" and "cafeteria Catholics."

The parish is now divided into those who support whatever the pastor and the design consultant say and those who oppose the renovation process and its expected results. The consultant aims to make parishioners feel guilty and, if they are resisting his archi-liturgical propaganda they are made to feel they are being "divisive," working against "unity in the parish" and against "creating a sense of community." This psychological pressure is often very effective in marginalizing those who dissent from the archi-liturgical status quo. Some will get so upset with the dishonesty and deceit that they no longer return to participate in the remaining sessions. The renovation process is specifically designed to wear out the opposition, so that by the time it comes to the "decision-making" part of the process only the docile sheep of the parish remain.

However, a few educated, daring and motivated parishioners may choose to remain "in the process" and appeal to their bishop or form groups[53] to work together to

---

acts like a decision, it must be a decision. The second reason not to accept this saying is that if you remain silent until the decisions have been made it will be too late to change anything" (*The Parishioner*, newsletter of the St. Francis Xavier Historic Preservation Guild, March 22, 1999).

[53] In March of 1999, parishioners who want to preserve St. Francis for future generations formed an association called the St. Francis Xavier Historic Preservation Guild, with 12 parishioners taking the lead. The Guild publishes a newsletter that is distributed to their more than 600

get the process and the renovation project halted. Appeals to the bishop, however, are often answered with a form letter that states that he trusts the pastor to make sound pastoral decisions during the renovation project, and advises parishioners to accept their pastor's decisions even though they may not agree with them.[54]

The marginalization[55] process continues as long as necessary. The vocal group opposing renovation plans—sometimes a formally organized preservation guild—will invariably be castigated publicly in homilies and in parish newsletters and bulletins. The sole purpose of this is to vilify the opposition as fringe dissidents in order to discredit them and their criticisms, while portraying

---

members, uniting them in their common cause. Charitable, succinct and informative, *The Parishioner* clarifies much of the misinformation put forth by the design consultant and has effectively exposed the manipulative and unethical process she uses to psychologically pressure her clients into accepting her preordained plan for the archi-liturgical future of their church. The Guild also sponsors "open forum" nights. These public meetings have provided parishioners with an opportunity to honestly voice their concerns, something they were not able to do at the consultant's educational sessions. They also invited a series of guest speakers to address issues regarding building codes, the rights of the laity, and the processes that other churches have undergone in similar situations.

[54] "In late December [1994], the Parishioners for Preserving Our Historic St. Mary's Church [in Mt. Angel, Oregon] began circulating petitions, hoping to stop the 'renovation.' Within a few weeks they had gathered signatures from 380 families—a number which has now grown to more than 600—out of the parish of 800... Members of the association also began writing to Archbishop [William] Levada, beseeching him to intervene. Levada supported the pastor, and suggested that if critics of the renovation could not support it, they "refrain from actions which serve only to divide the parish and impede the pastor and dedicated parishioners from accomplishing their important goal" (*The Wanderer*, Aug. 17, 1995).

[55] Bishop Thomas J. Tobin of Youngstown, Oh., wrote in one of his newspaper columns that "Church leaders need to address well-founded complaints seriously, or we will continue to see the marginalization of many good people who just care about the spiritual well-being of the Church" (*The Catholic Exponenet*, "Without a Doubt").

them and their criticisms, while portraying renovation proponents as victims of intolerant and rigid people.[56] Further, it is not uncommon for members of the parish

---

[56] During the renovation of St. Philip Church in Morrow, Ohio, members of the construction crew discovered that 15 wedgebolts that were holding together concrete formwork had been "removed" during the night. An article in *The Cincinnati Enquirer* ("Warren church rift behind sabotage?" May 6, 1999) stated that the construction site had been sabotaged by renovation protestors. "Pastor Joseph Allison said he suspects the sabotage had something to do with the expansion. He said about 50 of the conservative parish's 500 families have publicly opposed the expansion. The project includes a lowered altar in the center of the sanctuary, a side chapel for the tabernacle, upholstered chairs with kneelers to replace the pews, and offices on the lower level... 'I don't know whether they are involved, but it certainly puts them on the firing line,' he said. In this case the pastor is suggesting that renovation protestors may likely be guilty of attempted murder. If the formwork would have collapsed "it would have sent four or five or six people to the hospital or the graveyard," the foreman of the construction company told the *Enquirer*. Whereas the suggestion—that critics of the renovation sabotaged the construction site in the dark of the night—is ludicrous, renovation proponents did not hesitate to spread the slander in a major newspaper. In other words, renovation critics were slandered as malicious and evil criminals. One of the members on the Historic Preservation Guild at St. Philip's told a friend what had happened. Her friend, who owns a construction company and has years of experience with concrete formwork, told her that it would have been humanly impossible for anyone to remove the wedgebolts from the formwork without dissembling it at the same time. It is not uncommon, he said, for workers at a construction site to forgot to put the wedgebolts in place as they construct the formwork.

Also at St. Philip, rumors of death threats against the pastor persistently circulated. When anti-renovation parishioners wrote to their archbishop, he would respond to each of them addressing the rumor that someone had issued a "death threat" to the pastor. This went on for months, until the pastor was confronted about the alleged death threat. Although for months he made no attempt to clarify the rumor, he admitted, when asked, that he was unaware of any such death threats against him. It evidently suited his purpose to be perceived as a victim.

pastoral council or staff to be dismissed because they are unwilling to support the proposed renovation.[57]

Phase 4 – Renovation bureaucracy initiated

By this time the pastor has identified those in the parish who will be strong advocates of the predetermined plan for the renovation. These parishioners are placed on the "re-vision" or "renew" committees to stack the deck against those who oppose the project. Some consultants recommend a complex bureaucratic structure. For example, there may be a finance committee, fundraising committee, logistics and hospitality committee, data gathering committee, architect selection committee, publicity and communications committee, art and furnishings committee, music instruments committee, and liturgy committee.[58]

Each of these committees then works with the consultant, the pastoral staff and parish council. The whole proc-

---

[57] "In the continuing effort to 'sack' St. Philip Church in Morrow, Ohio, three parishioners who pro-actively opposed the church renovation plans there were fired from their positions on the parish council. A fourth council member voluntarily resigned when asked to do so by St. Philip pastor, Fr. J.C. Allison. When asked if they would continue to oppose the church renovation, Lois Westerheide, Roseann Siderits, Marion Ackman, and Carvel Steinke all said that they would. Siderits explained that her pastor expected all council members to support what she believes is the full-scale gutting of the church interior. 'We on the parish council are supposed to represent the parish,' commented Lois Westerheide. The parish is divided. Many parishioners have voiced objections to the proposal, yet every time parishioners—including members of council and the renovation steering committee—expressed their concern about the project, they were ignored.' Siderits said she felt that the proposal was not one that would promote unity within the parish, and according to the 'roles and procedures for parish council' distributed by Fr. Allison, members of council are "to be the eyes and ears to the hopes, concerns and needs of parishioners, as well as any particular group or organization in the parish" (St. Catherine Review, Sept./Oct., 1998).

[58] Father Vosko's motto for his committees is "More people doing less."

ess is often outlined in an advanced planning packet, which details the inner workings of the process for those who will be helping—whether they know it or not—with the smoke-and-mirrors.

The committee structure helps forge the impression that the whole project design process is democratic and a community effort. Each committee is charged with special tasks designed to promote the renovation program. For instance, the "publicity and communications committee" is responsible for announcing the renovation process through a specially designed newsletter, publicizing the renovation effort through local media, placing bulletin and pulpit announcements each weekend, and inserting the FDLC "educational inserts" into the weekly bulletin. The committee may also be asked to arrange media interviews with community leaders and the consultant if possible.

Phase 5 – Small groups design workshop

Parishioners are then questioned by means of an anonymous survey as to how they feel about their faith, and the church itself. They are probed about what they think is wrong with the building, what they would like to see included in the new design, etc. The information gathered from the surveys is then used to lead parishioners to the conclusion that the parish is not celebrating the sacraments according to the "spirit of Vatican II" and that a remodeled church (or even a new church) is necessary to meet the needs of the new liturgy.

A "design workshop" with a catchy title such as "God's House is Our House Too!" is held at the parish. This is the summit of the process. The workshop is advertised as "a chance to share our ideas for our worship facility with each other." Parishioners are broken up into small groups of seven or eight people. Each group has its own facilitator drawn from the pastor's hand-picked committees. The group facilitators attempt to steer the parishioners to discuss preset issues with the hope that their group will ultimately adopt the consultant's archi-liturgical ideas as their own.

There might be six or seven out of the eight people in a small group that do *not* accept the consultant's plan one bit. Yet if the appointed leader has been coached or indoctrinated to promote the consultant's program, then that person could end up speaking for the entire group, recommending the exact opposite of what the group near-unanimously feels.[59]

Even when the change agent is either unsuccessful or unavailable to domineer, the small group process is still designed to produce the intended result. At the conclusion of the design workshop, each small group advances its design agenda—what they want. The consultant then compiles the "input." Only the pastor and the consultant know the results. A couple of weeks later, upon the consultant's return to town, it is announced that the parish has "chosen" the preordained plan advocated all along by the design consultant.

Commenting on the Delphi Technique in *Education Reporter*, Lynn Stuter called this "small groups" input session "the crux" of the process. "If 50 people write down their

---

[59] At St. Mary's Church in Mount Angel, Oregon, "there were four meetings of parishioners to discuss changes. Parishioners were broken into eight to twelve small groups of nine or ten parishioners each. The first two meetings discussed non-controversial issues involved in the restoration, but the third meeting, recalls [parishioner Tim] Farris, was different. "That's when the pastor brought up the idea of moving the altar into the center of the church and that's when we noticed the leaders were not acting as advocated. One of the leaders told us the altar was going to be changed, and that there was nothing we could do about that. Then it became clear that when the group leaders would offer their summaries, they weren't reflecting what the other members were saying. The leaders tried to give the impression that only a few people opposed the change, when the consensus in the majority of groups was actually opposed" (*The Wanderer*, Aug. 17, 1995).

ideas individually, to be compiled later into a final outcome, no one knows what anyone else has written. That the final outcome of such a meeting reflects anyone's input at all is highly questionable."[60]

Phase 6 – Implementation

From this point on the core committee hand-picked by the pastor sees the project as smoothly as possible to its completion. Sometimes, however, one or two of those elected to the executive renovation committee get in the way of the process. They may even oppose the renovation plans that eventually unfold. For these few it is rough-going. They are ignored.[61] Some are dismissed from the committee if they become too vocal. Others cannot stand the pressure and resign. The whole process is designed to wear out the opposition, so that by the time it comes to make the final "decisions" only renovation proponents and docile sheep remain.

The preordained plan is trotted out and ratified. Consensus is reached and the project is implemented.

---

[60] Stuter, Lynn. "Focus: Using the Delphi Technique to Achieve Consensus," *Education Reporter,* November, 1998.

[61] "'I was genuinely interested in being an effective member of the decision-making committee,' said [Eric] Greyerbiehl. He thought he could best do this by listening to the parishioners he was supposed to represent. 'We have repeatedly been told tat this is the listening phase of the process' but it is becoming clearer, he says, that 'we're only supposed to listen to certain people" (*The Wanderer,* Sept. 9, 1999).

CHAPTER 3

The Professional Renovator's Repertoire
Resources Recommended by
the Liturgical Design Consultant

ೞಉಅ

FOR THOSE INTERESTED in immersing themselves in the rhetoric of the liturgical design consultant, this chapter should be of some interest. It lists the chief archi-liturgical resources recommended to parishioners during the "education" sessions that initiate the church renovation process.

Of special note are the periodicals geared toward liturgists and liturgical design consultants. The best way to become familiar with the fads and techniques of liturgists and design consultants is to request a few sample issues of each journal listed below. Study these and investigate the various claims that are made within.

Another source of indispensable information regarding trends and fads in the archi-liturgical world is your diocesan Office of Worship. Many dioceses issue newsletters that keep the diocesan liturgists all thinking about the same subjects at the same time. If you have ever wondered why you can walk into parishes in different cities of the same diocese during Lent to find a plastic snake in sand instead of holy water in the fonts, or why the same tacky banners seem to appear in the sanctuary at Christmas, the Office of Worship's newsletter is the explanation. The Archdiocese of Cincinnati's quarterly newsletter, *Worship,* is typical. It includes reprinted articles from some of the national liturgical journals listed below and a question-and-answer section addressing such burning questions as "Why do we have to move the tabernacle from our main worship space to a separate chapel when we build our churches?" Workshops and conferences are advertised, books reviewed, ideas exchanged.

Documents

Bishops' Committee on the Liturgy, *Environment and Art in Catholic Worship,* Washington DC: NCCB/USCC Publications Office, 1978.

Canadian Conference of Catholic Bishops, "A House for the Church: Font of Life." *National Bulletin on Liturgy.* May-June, 1980.

Books

Apostolos-Cappadona, D., ed. *Art, Creativity, and the Sacred: An Anthology in Religion and Art.* New York: Crossroad, 1984.

Bouyer, Louis. *Liturgy and Architecture.* Notre Dame, IN: University of Notre Dame Press, 1967.

Brown, Bill, ed. *Building and Renovation Kit for Places of Catholic Worship.* Chicago: Liturgy Training Publications, 1982.

Clowney, Paul & Tessa. *Exploring Churches.* Grand Rapids, MI: Wm. B. Eerdmans, Publishing Co., 1982.

Davies, J.G. *Temples, Churches and Mosques: A Guide to the Appreciation of Religious Architecture.* New York: Pilgrim Press, 1983.

Debuyst, Frederick. *Modern Architecture and Christian Celebration.* Richmond, VA: John Knox Press, 1968.

Huck, Gabe. *Liturgy with Style and Grace.* Chicago: Liturgy Training Publications, 1984.

Kennedy, Roger. *American Churches.* New York: Stewart, Tabori & Chang Publishers, Inc., 1982.

Lathrop, Gordon W. *Holy Things: A Liturgical Theology.* Minneapolis, MN: Fortress Press, 1993.

Lynn, Edward. *Tired Dragons: Adapting Church Architecture to Changing Needs.* Boston, MA: Beacon Press, 1972.

Mauck, Marchita. *Shaping a House for the Church.* Chicago: Liturgy Training Publications, 1990.

Mauck, Marchita. *Places for Worship.* Collegeville, MN: The Liturgical Press, 1995.

McNally, Dennis. *Sacred Space: An aesthetic for the Liturgical Environment.* Bristol, IN: Wyndham Hall Press, 1985.

Purdy, Martin. *Churches and Chapels: A Design and Development Guide.* Boston MA: Butterworth Architecture, 1991.

Simons, Thomas. *The Ministry of the Liturgical Environment.* Collegeville, MN: The Liturgical Press, 1984.

Sövik, Edward A., ed. *Accessible Church Buildings.* New York: United Church Board For Homeland Ministries, 1980.

Sövik, Edward A. *Architecture for Worship.* Minneapolis, MN: Augsburg Publishers, 1973.

Tillich, Paul. *On Art and Architecture.* John and Jane Dillenberger, editors. New York: Crossroad, 1989.

Vosko, Richard. *Through the Eye of A Rose Window: A Perspective on the Environment for Worship.* San Jose, CA: Resource Publications, 1981.

Walton, Janet. *Art and Worship: A Vital Connection.* Collegeville, MN: The Liturgical Press, (no date).

White, James and Susan. *Church Architecture: Building and renovating for Christian Worship.* Nashville, TN: Abingdon Press, 1988.

White, Susan. *Art, Architecture and Liturgical Reform.* New York: Pueblo Publishing Co., 1990.

Periodicals

Assembly. Notre Dame Center for Pastoral Liturgy. PO Box 81, Notre Dame, IN 46556.

Environment & Art Letter. (Monthly newsletter). Liturgy Training Publications, 1800 N Hermitage Ave., Chicago, IL 60622-1101

FDLC Newsletter. Federation of Diocesan Liturgical Commissions, 401 Michigan Ave NE, PO Box 29039, Washington, DC 20017

Faith and Forum. (Quarterly magazine). Interfaith Forum on Religion, Art and Architecture, 1777 Church St., Washington, DC 20036.

Liturgy. The Liturgical Conference, 1017 12th St NW, Washington, DC 20005.

Liturgy 90. Liturgy Training Publications, 1800 N Hermitage Ave., Chicago, IL 60622-1101.

Ministry & Liturgy (formerly *Modern Liturgy*). Resource Publications, 160 E Virginia St, Suite 290, San Jose, CA 95112.

Handouts
LDCs and their cohorts love indoctrination handouts. The following are the most popular:

Three bulletin inserts: "The Blessed Sacrament: Past and Current Practice." FDLC, Box 816, Ben Franklin Station, Washington, DC 20044. Phone: (202) 635-6991

Single bulletin insert: "Your Parish Church: How Should It Look Today?" Thomas Richstatter, OFM. Catholic Update, Issue No. UDP 110. St, Anthony Messenger Press, 1615 Republic St., Cincinnati, OH 45210. Phone: 1-800-488-0488.

Single bulletin insert: "A Tour of a Catholic Church." Thomas Richstatter, OFM. Catholic Update, Issue No. CO391. St. Anthony Messenger Press, 1615 Republic St. Cincinnati, OH 45210. Phone: 1-800-488-0488.

Eleven bulletin inserts on church interiors: Andrew Ciferni, O. Praem., and George Yu. FDLC, Box 816, Ben Franklin Station, Washington, DC 20044. Phone: (202) 635-6991

Magazine and journal articles are also often reproduced to serve as handouts to a congregation undergoing the church renovation process. The following three authors appear to be the most prolific on the subject of church renovation and design:

Brown, Bill: Promoter of the "Client Happiness Curve," Brown's writings often focus on such practical items as the building/renovation process, hiring an architect, and fundraising. His articles have appeared in *Environment and Art Letter* (e.g. "Sources of Funds," April, 1988), *Liturgy* (e.g., "The Process of Building," Spring, 1986, in which he states that the process begins with a plea to build trusting relationships within the community), and *Assembly* (e.g., "Client-Centered Architecture," November, 1987). He is also editor of the *Building and Renovation Kit for Places of Catholic Worship* published by Liturgical Training Publications.

Buscemi, John: This liturgical design consultant has published numerous articles in publications such as *U.S. Catholic, Assembly, Today's Parish* (e.g. "Catholics should look like the Cross," Oct, 1989), *Pastoral Music* (e.g., "Creating the Sacred: Participation in Art," April-May, 1983), and *Environment and Art Letter* (e.g. "Viewpoint: Kneelers?" August, 1990).

Ciferni, Fr. Andrew: Father Ciferni is another well-known archi-liturgical consultant. He has had pertinent articles published by the Federation of Diocesan Liturgical Commissions, *Pastoral Music* (e.g., "Buildings that Say 'Welcome'," June-July, 1989), *Environment and Art Letter* (e.g.,

"Eucharistic Reservation and Music Ministry Spaces,"
March, 1989), and *Assembly* (e.g., "Christian Table Eti-
quette: A Spirituality of the Altar," May, 1989).

Mauk, Marchita B: Art historian and liturgical consultant
Marchita Mauk has published articles in *Liturgy* (c.g.,
"Buildings that House the Church," Spring, 1986), *New
Catholic World* (e.g., "The Environment for Worship,"
March/April, 1987), *Assembly* (e.g., "What's in a Church?"
November, 1987), and *Environment and Art Letter* ("The
Cross at Liturgy," Sept. 1991).

Directory

The Federation of Diocesan Liturgical Commissions,
Liturgical Consultants for Worship Space. Washington, DC:
FDLC, various publication dates. (This is a regularly up-
dated directory of "liturgical design consultants" covering
fee structures, philosophy, credentials. To order your copy,
contact the FDLC at 401 Michigan Ave NE, PO Box 29039,
Washington DC 20017.)

CHAPTER 4

Challenging the Liturgical Design Consultant
How to Respond to Renovation Rhetoric

ഐരൾ

IN THE COURSE OF FACILITATING the renovation process, liturgical design consultants (LDCs) and liturgists will often make statements like those in this chapter. Following each hypothetical statement, a response is provided that challenges the erroneous or misleading information which it contains. The responses rely heavily on authoritative Church teaching and discipline, refer to relevant Church documents or statements, and include reflections on the various topics by individual bishops, priests and others.

1. "Environment and Art in Catholic Worship"

LDC's Statement: The 1978 document "Environment and Art in Catholic Worship" is an authoritative document that mandates certain changes when parishes undertake a renovation project. These directives must be followed.

Response: That statement is false. According to Father James Moroney, director of the bishops' Committee on Liturgy, "'Environment and Art in Catholic Worship' is a

1978 statement of the Bishops' Committee on the Liturgy. The purpose of the document is to provide principles for those involved in preparing liturgical space. The committee statement received the approval of the Administrative Committee in keeping with Conference policy. Because the document was not proposed as a statement of the whole conference of Bishops, the full body of bishops was never asked to consider it.

"'Environment and Art in Catholic Worship' does not have the force of law in and of itself. It is not particular law for the dioceses of the United States of America, but a commentary on that law by the Committee for the Liturgy. However, it does quote several documents of the Apostolic See and in that sense it has the force of the documents it quotes in the areas where those documents legislate. The Bishops' Committee on the Liturgy has appointed a task group to revisit 'Environment and Art in Catholic Worship.' The Committee on the Liturgy intends to submit the revised edition of this document as a statement of the Conference of Bishops. It is therefore anticipated that the revised document will be considered by the full body of Bishops.[62]

LDC's Statement: *Even if I concede that the 1978 version of "Environment and Art in Catholic Worship" is not an "approved" document, I must tell you that the bishops are now in the process of revising the document so that it can obtain the authoritative approval of all of the American bishops. I have seen the revised EACW, and it differs very little from the 1978 edition.*

Response: The new document is not a "revision." A completely new document is being drafted and will be issued. From the *National Catholic Register*:

---

[62] Moroney, Father James, Bishops' Committee on the Liturgy, NCCB, (http://www.nccbuscc.org/liturgy/q&a/environment/environment.htm).

"The Committee on Liturgy is in the process of drafting the new document which will address design issues for renovations and new church buildings. Father Moroney told the *Register* that the new document is not a 'revision' of Environment and Art but 'a completely new document.'

"The new document, which has been in the works now for two years and is not yet titled, is slated to be considered by the liturgy committee [in June]. It will be presented to the full body of bishops in November, and finally voted on in June 2000.

"Father Moroney clarified that this new document, unlike *Environment and Art*, will be issued as a statement from the entire body of the National Conference of Catholic Bishops, and therefore will carry the authority of a conference document."[63]

According to an earlier report from *Our Sunday Visitor*, Fr. Moroney "executive director of the bishops' Committee on Liturgy, gave a presentation at the conference about the committee's ongoing projects. He told *Our Sunday Visitor* that the new 'Environment and Art' document will not be a revision of the 1978 letter, but will replace that document. And unlike the 1978 letter—which was only the statement of one committee—the new 'Environment and Art' document is expected to be a statement of the entire bishops' conference."[64]

LDC's Statement: *A statement in the U.S. Appendix to the General Instruction of the Roman Missal (GIRM) directs that "Environment and Art in Catholic Worship" be followed when renovating churches or designing new ones.*

Response: Ian Rutherford, editor of the Catholic Liturgi-

---

[63] Rose, Michael S., "Bishops Drafting Guidelines on Churches," *National Catholic Register*, June 13-19, 1999.
[64] Carey, Ann, "A meeting of minds for liturgical renewal," *Our Sunday Visitor*, October 18, 1998.

cal Library, spoke with Father James Moroney, executive director of the bishops' Committee on Liturgy about the statement in the U.S. Appendix which says "Environment and Art in Catholic Worship" is to be followed.

According to the bishops' Committee on Liturgy, the U.S. Appendix to the General Instruction, n. 238, which says that the directives of EACW are to be applied in the U.S., means that "where it is *repeating* principles and directives found in authoritative documents, it is to be followed. Any new statements not from authoritative documents are simply commentary and are not binding."[65]

In other words, the authority of "Environment and Art" is limited to its quotations from authoritative documents. These quotations, however, do not endow EACW with an authority of its own.

LDC's Statement: "Environment and Art" has been accepted by the whole body of U.S. bishops as a teaching tool for the Church in the United States. These bishops fully support "Environment and Art in Catholic Worship."

Response: It is true that *some* bishops wholeheartedly embrace the commentary provided by EACW. Further, many of them implement that document as a set of directives to be fulfilled in the renovation of churches and the construction of new churches in their dioceses.

However, many U.S. bishops—including archbishops and cardinals—object to the recommendations made in that 1978 document. For instance, at the 1998 "Society for Catholic Liturgy Conference," Chicago archbishop Francis E. Cardinal George, O.M.I, offered his observations on EACW.

"Mistakes surfaced in EACW," he observed. "That document presented a 'division' between the 'static presence' of Jesus in the Eucharist at Mass and the 'reserved

---

[65] Catholic Liturgical Library, http://www.catholicliturgy.com

presence' of Jesus in the Blessed Sacrament in the tabernacle. EACW, in essence, relegated the Eucharist to a closet." Cardinal George predicted that this "directive" will not be in the new version of EACW.[66]

Cardinal George has been outspoken on numerous occasions voicing his objections to that 1978 document. At the November, 1998 NCCB conference he stated, "The 'Art and Environment' document... has... been elevated to a status beyond all comprehension. People who dismiss *Humanae Vitae* as just somebody's personal opinion will swear that we all must be guided by [EACW]."[67]

LDC's statement: As you read through EACW you will quickly discover that many theological and liturgical references are made to the Roman document, 'General Instruction of the Roman Missal,' clearly an official document of the Catholic Church. So contrary to what you may personally believe, the document is authoritative.

Response: The argument here is that a document which cites or references an authoritative document of the Church becomes authoritative itself. If that were so, then this book would become an authoritative Church document, which it is not.

2. The Tabernacle

LDC's Statement: The Pope wants all churches to create a separate chapel for the Tabernacle. Church documents make this very clear. According to the Pope's document, Eucharisticum mysterium: "It is ... recommended that, as far as possible, the tabernacle be

---

[66] Carey, Ann, "A meeting of minds for liturgical renewal," *Our Sunday Visitor,* October 18, 1998.
[67] Hitchcock, Helen Hull, "Bishops Mull Restructuring," *Adoremus Bulletin,* February, 1999.

placed in a chapel distinct from the middle or center part of the church."

Response: Liturgical law *allows* for the placement of the Blessed Sacrament in separate chapels in our churches, but there is no "mandate" that all new churches and renovated churches must create a so-called separate chapel for the reservation of the Blessed Sacrament. Both the *Catechism* and the *Code of Canon Law* make clear that locating a tabernacle on or behind the main altar always remains a valid option and is nowhere ruled out.

The LDC's quote from *Eucharisticum mysterium* above is taken out of context. The complete quote is: "The place in a church or oratory where the Blessed Sacrament is reserved in the tabernacle should be truly prominent. It ought to be suitable for private prayer so that the faithful may easily and fruitfully, by private devotion also, continue to honor Our Lord in this sacrament. It is therefore recommended that, as far as possible, the tabernacle be placed in a chapel distinct from the middle or center part of the church, above all in those churches where marriages and funerals take place frequently, and in places which are much visited for their artistic and historical treasures."[68]

The paragraph that follows repeats the instruction of the Vatican's 1964 *Inter Oecumenici:* "The Blessed Sacrament is to be reserved in a solid, burglar-proof tabernacle in the center of the high altar or on another altar if this is really outstanding and distinguished. Where there is a lawful custom, and in particular cases to be approved by the local Ordinary, the Blessed Sacrament may be reserved in some other place in the church, but it must be a very special place, having nobility about it, and it must be suitably decorated."[69]

---

[68] Sacred Congregation for Rites, *Eucharisticum Mysterium*, 1967, no. 53.
[69] Sacred Congregation for Rites, *Inter Oecumenici*, 1964, no. 95.

According to Msgr. Peter J. Elliott, "all the official instructions during and since the Second Vatican Council need to be interpreted in the light of Canon 938.2 of the *Code of Canon Law*, 1983: 'The tabernacle in which the blessed Eucharist is reserved should be sited in a distinguished place in a church or oratory, a place which is conspicuous, suitably adorned and conducive to prayer.'"[70]

Eucharisticum mysterium was one relevant directive leading up to this Canon. Other directives include the Vatican's 1973 instruction on Holy Communion and the Worship of the Eucharist Outside of Mass[71] and the 1969 *General Instruction of the Roman Missal* (GIRM).[72] Both of these documents *recommend* the separate chapel to facilitate private devotion, yet neither rules out the possibility of the Blessed Sacrament being reserved on the main altar.

It is important to note, however, that a decade later, the Vatican issued *Inaestimabile Donum,* which states: "The tabernacle in which the Eucharist is kept can be located *on an altar or away from it,* in a place in the church which is very prominent, truly noble and duly decorated, or in a chapel suitable for private prayer and for adoration of the faithful."[73]

Msgr. Elliott explains the development within these directives: "we see first of all that *Inaestimabile Donum* modifies the favor for a separate eucharistic chapel in GIRM, no. 276. In the decade separating the two instructions, problems had arisen with a diminution of devotion to the Eucharist, not dissociated from inadequate attention to the place of reservation in new or renovated churches. This may explain why Canon 938.2 seems to reflect the mind of

---

[70] Elliott, Msgr. Peter J., *Ceremonies of the Modern Roman Rite,* San Francisco: Ignatius Press, 1995, Appendix 9.

[71] Sacred Congregation for Divine Worship, *Eucharisticae Sacramentum,* 1973, Introduction, no. 9.

[72] *General Instruction of the Roman Missal,* 1969, no. 276.

[73] Sacred Congregation for Divine Worship, *Inaestimabile Donum,* 1980, no. 24.

Inaestimabile Donum more than GIRM and the instructions on eucharistic worship. Can 938.2 is not a mere synthesis of previous instructions. It corrects misinterpretations of those rules... We also see that locating a tabernacle on an altar always remains a valid option and is nowhere ruled out."[74]

The only command that the tabernacle may not be kept on an altar comes from the non-authoritative "Environment and Art in Catholic Worship," in paragraph 80: "The tabernacle... may be placed in a wall niche, on a pillar, eucharistic tower. It should not be placed on an altar for the altar is a place for action not reservation."[75] This is used as the rationale to move the Blessed Sacrament away from the altar (although traditionally the tabernacle is located, not *on* the altar itself, but behind it). No authoritative Church documents provide any sort of rationale for removing the tabernacle, much less a rationale remotely resembling these reasons.

LDC's statement: *Vatican II requires that the tabernacle be moved off of the high altar to another position in the church to facilitate proper celebration of the new rites.*

Response: This statement says much the same as the previous one, and thus the previous response applies here. A letter from Cardinal Joseph Ratzinger, prefect for the Congregation for the Doctrine of the Faith to Bishop Laurence Ryan of Carlow, Ireland, clarifies the position that no liturgical legislation in the period after Vatican II mandates that the tabernacle be moved from the high altar to another position in the church.

---

[74] Elliott, Msgr. Peter J., *Ceremonies of the Modern Roman Rite*, San Francisco: Ignatius Press, 1995, , Appendix 9.
[75] Bishops Committee on Liturgy, *Environment and Art in Catholic Worship*, 1978, no. 80.

Cardinal Ratzinger writes: "I could not but acknowledge that in this legislation there exists no mandate, in the primary sense of the term as a command or an order, to move the tabernacle from the high altar to another position in the church. With respect to the placement of the tabernacle, the instruction *Inter Oecumenici* (1964) par. 95, which implemented the decisions of *Sacrosanctum Consilium*, states quite clearly that the Blessed Sacrament be reserved on the high altar, a possibility envisaged also by *Eucharisticum Mysterium* (1967), par. 54... It is certainly true that a great number of churches since the Second Vatican Council have been re-arranged; such changes, while inspired by the liturgical reform, cannot, however, be said to have been required by the legislation of the Church."[76]

LDC's statement: *Adoration of the Eucharist is opposed to the celebration of Mass.*

Response: Bishop Thomas J. Tobin of Youngstown addresses this contention in his 1998 pastoral on the centrality of the Eucharist: He writes:

"Some have maintained that the promotion of the adoration of the Blessed Sacrament will take away from the centrality of the Eucharistic celebration. It need not do so. In fact, proper devotion to the Blessed Sacrament will inevitably lead to a fuller participation in the Eucharistic celebration: 'Outside the Eucharistic celebration, the Church is careful to venerate the Blessed Sacrament, which must be reserved... as the spiritual center of the religious and parish community. Contemplation prolongs communion and enables one to meet Christ, true God and true man, in a lasting way... Prayer of adoration in the presence of the Blessed Sacrament unites the faithful with the paschal mystery; it enables them to share in Christ's sacri-

---

[76] Caesar, Bernard, "Cardinal Ratzinger on the Question of Sanctuary Renovations," *AD2000*, October, 1998.

fice, of which the Eucharist is the permanent sacrament'."[77]

In an interview with architect Duncan Stroik, Abbot Boniface Luykx, a Vatican II *peritus* and member of the Concilium (the group charged with implementing the liturgical reforms of Vatican II), had this to say: "The tabernacle's function is as an extension of the Mass. Our personal prayer of adoration before the Blessed Sacrament is in continuity with the Mass, in participation with it, in desire if we cannot go. What Christ is doing in the tabernacle is offering himself to the Father, just as in the Mass, and also wanting to nourish us in spiritual communion. He does something in the tabernacle, but it is in relation with the Mass."[78]

LDC's statement: The presence of the tabernacle behind the altar table causes confusion between devotion and the celebration of the Eucharist.

Response: The presence of the reserved Blessed Sacrament ought not cause confusion between devotion and the celebration of the Eucharist; rather, they complement one another. As Vatican II *peritus* Abbot Boniface Luykx stated in the previous response, "adoration (private devotion) before the Blessed Sacrament must always be carried out "in continuity with the Mass." In other words, he says, "we should not play out the altar against the tabernacle." Since the reserved Sacrament is an extension of the Mass, it logically follows that, architecturally speaking, the tabernacle ought to be situated in direct relationship to the altar, whether on the altar or away from it. Abbott Boniface

---

[77] John Paul II, 'Letter on the 750th Anniversary of the Feast of Corpus Christi,' no. 3.

[78] Rt. Rev. Archimandrite Boniface Luykx, "Liturgical Architecture: Domus Dei or Domus Ecclesiae," *Catholic Dossier*, May-June, 1997.

points out that "It is an unenlightened sacramental devotion to concentrate on the tabernacle *apart from the Mass.*"[79]

Bishop Thomas J. Tobin recommends that prayer before the Blessed Sacrament, "before and after Mass and on other private occasions, should be encouraged as a way of preparing for the celebration of the Eucharist and of extending its meaning."[80] It can hardly be expected that an entire congregation stuff itself into a small Blessed Sacrament chapel before and after each Mass. It stands to reason then that the tabernacle be kept in the sanctuary in a recognizable relationship with the altar.

Msgr. William Smith commented on the subject in *Homiletic & Pastoral Review*: "Frankly, I have never met an adult Catholic who was ever confused about celebration [of the Holy Sacrifice of the Mass] at the expense of reservation or vice versa. Centrally located and recognizable tabernacles never contributed to such confusion; indeed, where a recognizable tabernacle is visible it is immediately obvious to all that it is for reservation only!"[81]

LDC's statement: The cathedral in this diocese (or the Roman basilicas, etc.) has a separate chapel for the reservation of the Blessed Sacrament. If it is good enough for them, it ought to be good enough for you.

Response: "As indicated in the 1967 instruction *Eucharisticum Mysterium,* no. 53, and again as it is repeated in the 1973 document *Eucharisticae Sacramentum,* there are situations when a Blessed Sacrament chapel is appropriate, for example, in a cathedral or major church frequented by crowds of tourists or pilgrims, such as the Roman basilicas,

---

[79] Ibid.

[80] Tobin, Bishop Thomas J., *The Eucharist: To Be Loved, To Be Lived,* 1998.

[81] Smith, Msgr. William Smith, "Placement of the Tabernacle," *Homiletic & Pastoral Review,* December, 1998.

or where a safe place is required for perpetual adoration. The chapel may also be appropriate in the rare case where the tabernacle would seem very distant and inaccessible if placed at the back of a deep sanctuary. Moreover, the *Ceremonial of Bishops*, no. 49, citing a very ancient tradition, recommends a chapel for cathedrals."[82] Even here there is not a requirement for a private chapel, only a recommendation.

Just because a certain arrangement is recommended for a cathedral, a basilica, or some other large historic church does not mean that it is necessarily appropriate for a parish church. Following the LDC's rationale we could advocate also a separate baptistery, rows of statuary, a dozen side chapels, ornate high altars with reredos, etc., depending on the basilica or cathedral church we would like to copy.

LDC's statement: *If you go to a church in Europe you will notice that almost all the churches there have separate chapels for the Blessed Sacrament.*

Response: When most Americans visit Europe they tend to visit the large basilicas and cathedrals that are of great historical and artistic significance. These tend to be large churches that attract a fair amount of tourist traffic each day. For that reason, it is perfectly logical, because of either size or traffic, that these churches provide a separate chapel for the Blessed Sacrament.

Thus, the Blessed Sacrament "can" be kept "in a chapel suitable for private prayer and for adoration by the faithful." This is, for instance, a necessary option for pastors in historic cathedrals which are visited daily by tourists who may not convey the reverence due to the Blessed Sacrament. Since these cathedrals are also parishes, the parish-

---

[82] Elliott, Msgr. Peter J., *Ceremonies of the Modern Roman Rite*, San Francisco: Ignatius Press, 1995, Appendix 9.

ioners have a right to private prayer and worship of the Blessed Sacrament, and the Blessed Sacrament has every right to be respected. In those cases, there is a good reason to provide a side chapel for private worship of the Blessed Sacrament.

If one were to tour the parish churches in Europe one would find many of the traditional layouts (basilican form with tabernacle at the middle of a high altar) still intact. In other churches, one may find tacky renovations much as one might find in the United States and Canada.

LDC's statement: *Do you think that the Mass is less in a church that has a separate chapel for the reserved sacrament?*

Response: If Mass is validly and licitly celebrated, no, the Holy Sacrifice of the Mass itself would not be any "less" in a church that has a separate chapel for the reserved sacrament. However, if parishioners can be properly disposed and prepared for celebrating the Eucharist, they will be able to offer themselves more fully, united to the Holy Sacrifice of the Altar.

One of the best ways to prepare for Mass, as recommended by bishops as well as the Holy Father, is prayer before the Blessed Sacrament. Archbishop Theodore McCarrick of Newark, N.J. wrote in a pastoral letter on the Eucharist: "In new renovations permission is not granted to locate the tabernacle in a place where it is not visible by the great majority of the congregation. Most of our Catholic people can come into the church only for Sunday Mass. It would be a great loss for all of us if they were never conscious of the fact that the Lord is there reserved in the tabernacle for their adoration and their prayer. If they can never see the tabernacle, then their devotion to the Blessed Sacrament may soon begin to falter and decline.[83]

Likewise Bishop Thomas J. Tobin of Youngstown recommends that prayer before the Blessed Sacrament, "before and after Mass and on other private occasions, should be encouraged as a way of preparing for the celebration of the Eucharist and of extending its meaning."[84]

To facilitate this in the parish church the tabernacle must be located 1). in a place where the entire congregation is able to gather; and 2). in a strong relation to the altar of sacrifice. Thus, in churches that have the tabernacle situated behind the "high altar," in a reredos or beneath a baldachino, the tabernacle need not be move from that location.

Again, according to Abbot Boniface, "It is an unenlightened sacramental devotion to concentrate on the tabernacle apart from the Mass... We should not play out the altar against the tabernacle."[85]

LDC's statement: *The Church is being very "conservative" or "traditional" when it seeks to recover its ancient tradition which had a separate space for the Blessed Sacrament to be reserved. Its position in the main worship space is not an ancient tradition, it is a more recent tradition.*

Response: First of all, it is not the Church which is seeking to "recover its ancient tradition which had a separate space for the Blessed Sacrament." It is the archi-liturgical establishment which wants to do this for reasons which have nothing to do with Church tradition, history or liturgy. This is neither a "traditional" nor a "conservative" ap-

---

[83] McCarrick, Archbishop Theodore, "All Praise and All Thanksgiving: A Pastoral Letter on the Eucharist," *Religious Life*, October, 1995.

[84] Tobin, Bishop Thomas J., *The Eucharist: To Be Loved, To Be Lived*, 1998.

[85] Rt. Rev. Archimandrite Boniface Luykx, "Liturgical Architecture: Domus Dei or Domus Ecclesiae," *Catholic Dossier*, May-June, 1997.

proach. Such a statement only mocks those who seek to maintain continuity with 2000 years of the Christian faith and tradition.

Addressing problems that were arising in this regard as early as 1947, Pope Pius XII wrote in his encyclical on the Sacred Liturgy: "The liturgy of the early ages is most certainly worthy of all veneration. But ancient usage must not be esteemed more suitable and proper, either in its own right or in its significance for later times and new situations, on the simple ground that it carries the savor and aroma of antiquity."[86]

Pope Pius writes that, although it is appropriate to conduct research in the field of ancient liturgy to understand the meaning of ancient feasts, sacred texts, and ceremonies conducted on their occasion, "it is neither wise nor laudable to reduce everything to antiquity by every possible device. Thus, to cite some instances, one would be straying from the straight path were he to wish the altar restored to its primitive table form; were he to want black excluded as a color for the liturgical vestments; were he to forbid the use of sacred images and statues in Churches; were he to order the crucifix so designed that the divine Redeemer's body shows no trace of His cruel sufferings; and lastly were he to disdain and reject polyphonic music or singing in parts, even where it conforms to regulations issued by the Holy See."[87]

The Holy Father calls this "exaggerated and senseless" desire to return to some optimal moment in the past "antiquarianism," a heresy which gave rise to the illegal Council of Pistoria. "Unwise and mistaken is the zeal of one who in matters liturgical would go back to the rites and usage of antiquity, discarding the new patterns introduced by dispo-

---

[86] Pope Pius XII, *Mediator Dei*, 1947, no. 61.
[87] Ibid., no.62.

sition of divine Providence to meet the changes of circumstances and situation."[88]

The theological and symbolic connection between the tabernacle and the altar is an important one that should not be dismissed because certain archi-liturgical theories manifest this "exaggerated and senseless" desire to return to a previous age.

LDC's statement: The laity began to "resort to" adoration during the Middle Ages because they felt they could not participate in Mass. This is when Corpus Christi processions and other devotions became popular, to the detriment of the Mass.

Response: In his book on devotion to the Eucharist, Father Benedict Groeschel traces Eucharistic devotion to the 6th century, well before what most people think of as "the Middle Ages." Steven J. Schloeder in *Architecture in Communion* provides some early manifestations of Eucharistic devotion: "We know that by [the 4th century] the Eucharist was reserved in churches, sometimes on altars, where it was an object for adoration and personal devotion. Saint Gregory of Nazianzus tells the story of his sister, Gorgonia, who when seriously ill 'went before the altar' and reverenced the Eucharist for her healing."[89]

In the LDC's statement, he uses the tactic of setting the Mass against private Eucharistic devotions, as if they fought against one another for the attention of the faithful. There is no historical evidence that private Eucharistic devotions have ever detracted from the Mass.

Even today Pope John Paul II reminds us that "adoration of Christ in this sacrament of love must find expression in various forms of eucharistic devotion: personal prayer before the Blessed Sacrament, Hours of Adoration,

---

[88] Ibid., no. 63-4.
[89] Schloeder, Steven J. *Architecture in Communion*, San Francisco: Ignatius Press, 1998.

periods of exposition—short, prolonged and annual (Forty Hours)—eucharistic benediction, eucharistic congresses."[90]

LDC's statement: The Tabernacle or "sacrament tower" ought to be made of a transparent material such as glass so that we may see into the place of reservation.

Response: According to the Code of Canon Law: "The tabernacle in which the Eucharist is regularly reserved is to be immovable, made of solid and opaque material, and locked so that the danger of profanation may be entirely avoided."[91]

The Code reiterates several other Vatican instructions of the construction of the tabernacle. *Eucharisticum Mysterium* states that "The Blessed Sacrament should be reserved in a solid, inviolable tabernacle in the middle of the altar, or in a side altar, but in a truly prominent place."[92] Likewise the 1964 document on the implementation of Vatican II's Constitution on the Sacred Liturgy states, "The Blessed Sacrament is to be reserved in a solid, burglar-proof tabernacle in the center of the high altar or on another altar if this is really outstanding and distinguished."[93]

Designing a transparent sacrament tower to be built out of glass is merely an illicit fad. If you can break it open easily with a household hammer it does not meet the requirements of burglar-proof, solid, or opaque.

LDC's statement: Change is hard, but understand what the Church is asking for is not a diminution of your love for the Eucharist or your reverence and respect for the Eucharist. What this is all about is broadening our awareness of Christ's presence,

---

[90] Pope John Paul II, *Dominicae Cenae*, 1980.
[91] *Code of Canon Law*, 1983, can. 938 §3.
[92] Pope Paul VI, *Eucharisticum Mysterium*, 1967, no.54.
[93] Sacred Congregation of Rites, *Inter Oecumenici*, 1964, no. 95.

and deepening our reverence for every way that Christ is present,
not just in the tabernacle.

Response: This statement is made up of two valid points
and a non-sequitur. But of course the Church is not asking
for a diminution of our love for the Eucharist. And it is
true that Christ is present in many ways. Yet when this
point is rationally considered, few would argue that the
presence of the tabernacle in the sanctuary makes it difficult to see Christ in their neighbor, in the ordained minister, or in the Word as proclaimed from Holy Scripture
during Mass, as outlined in *Sacrosanctum Concilium*, no. 7.
Thus, the burden is now on the LDC to explain how removing the tabernacle from the sanctuary is going to
broaden our awareness of the other ways in which Christ is
present.

However, another point, far and away the most important, is ignored by the LDC; namely that in the Blessed
Sacrament of the Altar, Christ is present in a unique way
that Catholics have traditionally refer to as the "Real Presence."

LDC's statement: *We used to have Sunday Mass followed by*
Benediction of the Blessed Sacrament, which was "the big thing."
The emphasis was on the reserved sacrament. The Council and
post-conciliar documents specifically called out that the Mass is
first and reservation second. It is the Mass that is central, not the
tabernacle.

Response: The LDC's statement reiterates the canard, already exposed above, that the Holy Sacrifice of the Mass is
somehow in competition with the reserved Sacrament. To
refute it once again: In reality the "active" and "static"
forms of the Blessed Sacrament are complementary. Likewise, adoration of the Blessed Sacrament complements the
Holy Sacrifice of the Mass. The reservation of the Sacra-

ment enables the Mass to be extended. Just because Benediction may follow Mass does not mean in any way that Benediction is "central" to public worship. If any one thing is adequately understood by Catholics around the globe today, it is that the Holy Sacrifice of the Mass, the public worship of the Church, is the source and summit of the Christian life.

Pope John Paul II and his predecessors have long encouraged Eucharistic adoration, not as "the big thing," but as a private devotion that is beneficial to all as an extension of the Mass. In *Dominicae Cenae*, for instance, Pope John Paul II writes: "Jesus waits for us in this sacrament of love. Let us be generous with our time in going to meet Him in adoration and in contemplation that is full of faith and ready to make reparation for the great faults and crimes of the world. May our adoration never cease."[94]

LDC's statement: What we're dealing with here is not just a question of reverence towards the tabernacle ("the gold box") and the reserved sacrament. We're dealing with the broader reality of an awareness of spirituality in man, awareness of the presence of God in man.[95]

Response: The LDC seems to argue that if one is reverent to Christ in the Eucharist, one cannot be aware of the presence of Christ in man. This is variant of the stratagem opposing the tabernacle and the altar described above. The illogicality of the statement is manifest. If Christ in the Blessed Sacrament obscures "Christ in Man," will not Christ upon the altar obscure himself even more?

Father Rich Simon makes an excellent point regarding "reverence" in his June 24, 1997 letter to his parishioners

---

[94] Pope John Paul II, *Dominicae Cenae*, 1980, no. 3.
[95] A direct quote from Father Lawrence E. Mick's presentation to parishioners of St. Martin of Tours Church in Cheviot, Ohio, November 26, 1998.

at St. Thomas of Canterbury Church in Chicago. He writes:

I believe that much of the liturgical experiment that began thirty years ago has failed. We are not holier, nor more Christ centered now than we were then. In fact, we are facing a generation of young people who are largely lost to the Church because we have not given them the precious gift that is at the heart of Catholicism, that is, the Real Presence of Jesus. Mass has become simply a drama, a vehicle for whatever agenda is currently popular. The church building is no longer a place of encounter with the Lord but a sort of a social center, not a place of prayer, rather a place of chatter.

In many churches, including our own, the Tabernacle was moved from the center of the church to add emphasis to Mass and the presence of the Lord in the reception of Holy Communion. The experiment, however, has failed. We have lost the sense of the sacred that formerly was the hallmark of Catholic worship. The behavior of many in the church is outrageous. When Mass is over it is impossible to spend time in prayer. The noise level reaches the pitch that one would expect at a sporting event. The kiss of peace seems like New Year's Eve. Christ is forgotten on the altar. You may counter that He is present in the gathering of the Church, and though this is true, it should not detract from the Lord present on the altar. If the Lord is truly recognized in the congregation, it should serve to enhance the sacredness of the moment. This is simply not happening...

Therefore, I have decided to restore the Tabernacle to its former place in the middle of the sanctuary and to begin a campaign of re-education as to the sacredness of worship and the meaning of the Real Presence. This means that I will nag and nag until a sense of the sacred is restored. I will be reminding you that a respectful quiet will have to be maintained in church. Food and toys and socializing are welcome elsewhere, but the church is the place of an encounter with the

Living God. It will not be a popular policy, but this is unimportant.

I can hear one objection already. Where will the priest sit? I will sit where the priest has traditionally sat, over on the side of the sanctuary. Here as in many churches the "presider's" chair was placed where the Tabernacle had been. I am sick of sitting on the throne that should belong to my Lord. The dethronement of the Blessed Sacrament has resulted in the enthronement of the clergy, and I for one am sick of it. The Mass has become priest-centered. The celebrant is everything. I am a sinner saved by grace as you are and not the center of the Eucharist. Let me resume my rightful place before the Lord rather than instead of the Lord. I am ordained to the priesthood of Christ in the order of presbyter, and as such I do have a special and humbling role. I am elder brother in the Lord and with you I seek to follow Him and to worship. Please, please let me return Christ to the center of our life together where He belongs.[96]

Once Fr. Simon returned the tabernacle to its former location at the center of the sanctuary, behind the altar he was surprised, he said, at the response. It was overwhelmingly positive and effective. Some sense of reverence was indeed restored at Mass in his church. On September 16, 1999 he reported the results of the move in a "form letter":

You cannot imagine the response I got to the letter I addressed to my parishioners on June 24th. I have gotten so many calls and letters that I am reduced to saying thank you in a form letter. Still, I simply have to write to say thank you for your support and prayers. So many people thought I was brave to do what I did. Brave? I simply read the Catechism and moved a few pieces of

---

[96] Simon, Fr. Rich, Letter to the parishioners of St. Thomas of Canterbury Parish, Chicago, Ill., June 24, 1997.

furniture. The response has been overwhelmingly positive. In the parish, some people even wept for joy when
they saw the change. I am still kicking myself and asking why I didn't do this years ago. The response has
been so supportive. Many wrote and expressed their
sense of loneliness in the battle for Catholic orthodoxy.
Well, you are not alone, neither among the laity nor the
clergy.

Perhaps you have heard the definition of a neo-
conservative. He is a liberal who has been mugged by
reality. That certainly describes me. I was in college in
the late Sixties and went the whole route: beard, san-
dals, protest, leafleting for feminism, and all the rest...
[I]f a parish like this and a person like me can be
turned from foolish liturgical experimentation, it can
happen anywhere to anyone. Don't give up! For instance, if they have taken the kneelers out of your
church, go to the front and kneel on the hard floor.
You'll be amazed how many will join you. That's what's
happened here.

LDC's statement: *"Eucharist" is not a noun; it is a verb. It is
something we do.*

Response: Simply referencing the *Catechism of the Catholic
Church*, we find that the Eucharist is defined as: "the source
and summit of the Christian life"(1325); "the efficacious
sign and sublime cause of that communion in the divine
life and that unity of the People of God by which the
Church is being kept" (1325); "the sum and summary of
our faith" (1327); "the memorial of the Lord's Passion and
Resurrection" (1330); "the sacrament of our salvation accomplished by Christ on the cross" (1359); "a sacrifice of
praise and thanksgiving for the work of creation" (1359);
"the memorial of Christ's Passover" (1362); etc.

Thus, the *Catechism* defines the Eucharist as source,
summit, sign, sum, summary, memorial, sacrament, and

sacrifice. Each of these words is of course a noun, not a verb.

Liturgists and design consultants are wont to redefine "Eucharist" to serve their own agenda. They often say things such as "let's Eucharist" or "when the Christian assembly gathers together for worship, it eucharists. The ramifications of treating the Eucharist as "something you do" are countless. The liturgical establishment has labored for years to redefine the Eucharist as such. They have done so because they do not want to acknowledge the sacrificial aspect of the Eucharist, nor do they want to emphasize the Real Presence of Jesus in the Blessed Sacrament, something which is definitely a noun, not a verb.

3. The Altar

LDC's statement: Moving the altar into the midst of the congregation encourages "community" and "active participation."

Response: Moving the altar into the midst of the people is neither mandated nor recommended in any authoritative Church document. What is meant by "community" and "active participation"? Any authentic Catholic community ought to be centered around the Eucharist and intimately united with the universal Church. The term "active participation" is widely misunderstood. In the official Latin version uses the term *actuosa participatio*. The term *actuosa* incorporates both the "contemplative" (internal) and "active" (external) aspects of participation. *Activa*, which also means active, normally excludes the contemplative aspect. The choice of *actuosa* instead of *activa* is significant.

In liturgy, as in our daily Christian lives, both the contemplative and the active complement each other. How do we foster both in a setting that still retains the mystery of the Eucharist, and the hierarchical nature of the Mass and the Church? How is *actuosa participatio*—both the contemplative and active aspects—fostered by throwing the altar into the midst of the congregation? Some have adduced evidence that it does not.

Abbot Boniface Luykx, one of the authors of Vatican II's *Constitution on the Sacred Liturgy*, believes that one of the main weaknesses of our Post-Conciliar churches is "the altar thrown into the midst of the people without protection of its holiness."[97] This practice erodes the symbolic value representing the hierarchical nature of the Church. Pope John Paul II said in his October 9, 1998 *ad limina* address to a group of American bishops: "The liturgy, like the Church, is intended to be hierarchical and polyphonic, respecting the different roles assigned by Christ and allowing all the different voices to blend in one great hymn of praise."

According to *Sacrosanctum Concilium* liturgy is primarily a form of worship, the "summit toward which the activity of the Church is directed."[98] Yet "the sacred liturgy does not exhaust the entire activity of the Church."[99] Building "community" through innovations in the liturgy and in the place of worship are mere gimmicks. The essential element in the community of Christians is their shared faith. Without this there is no community at all. Authentic "community" will build on this shared faith through faithful celebration of the liturgy, through hearing and preaching the Word of God, through catechesis, through embracing the Christian life.

LDC's statement: The Christians of the early Church (prior to the conversion of Constantine) did not celebrate Mass on the tombs of the martyrs in the catacombs. They simply broke bread

---

[97] Rt. Rev. Archimandrite Boniface Luykx, "Liturgical Architecture: Domus Dei or Domus Ecclesiae," *Catholic Dossier,* May-June, 1997.
[98] Pope Paul VI, *Sacrosanctum Concilium,* 1963, no.10.
[99] Pope Paul VI, *Sacrosanctum Concilium,* 1963, no.9.

around their dining room tables at a "house church" (or "home church").

Response: This statement is so controverted that sifting to the bottom for the facts could be a book in itself. However, there is more than ample evidence to suggest that tombs of the martyrs played an important part in the celebration of the Mass in the early Church.

The LDC's statement aims to disparage the use of stone altars and the placement of relics within the altar. Archeological evidence proves that the early Christians did use stone altars in the catacombs. However, they also used wooden altar for a number of centuries. As the Church developed her liturgy and theology, stone altars began to replace the wooden altars from the 6th century until they were practically universal in the 12th century. In 1596 the Church required that all altars be made of stone.

According to the GIRM this requirement is still normative, although other materials are permitted: "According to the traditional practice of the Church and the meaning of the altar, the table of a fixed altar should be of natural stone, but any solid, becoming, and skillfully constructed material may be used with the approval of the conference of bishops."[100] This is reiterated in the 1983 Code of Canon Law, which recommends that "the table of a fixed altar is to be of stone, in fact of a single natural stone."[101]

The *General Instruction* also reiterates that "It is fitting to maintain the practice of enclosing relics in the altar or of placing them under the altar."[102]

Notwithstanding the statements in GIRM and the Code the past 35 years have seen a proliferation of wooden tables used as altars. Liturgists have promoted their use because, they say, the wooden table resembles the dining-

---

[100] *General Instruction of the Roman Missal,* 1973, no. 263.
[101] *Code of Canon Law,* 1983, can. 1236.
[102] *General Instruction of the Roman Missal,* 1973, no. 266.

room table and better symbolizes gathering for a common meal. This is plainly at odds with the Church's actual teaching. Fifteen years before the Council, Pope Pius XII warned that "one would be straying from the straight path were he to wish the altar restored to its primitive table-form."

The problem with using a simple table is that at this stage in the development of the Church it is apt to be taken for a table rather than an altar. Its use is understood as signifying a change in sacramental theology.

LDC's statement: Our model for a Christian church is the dining room.

Response: According to the *Catechism of the Catholic Church,* paragraph 1181 describes the church building as "a house of prayer in which the Eucharist is celebrated and reserved, where the faithful assemble, and where is worshipped the presence of the Son of God our Savior, offered for us on the sacrificial altar for the help and consolation of the faithful—this house ought to be in good taste and a worthy place for prayer and sacred ceremonial. In this 'house of God' the truth and harmony of the signs that make it up should show Christ to be present and active in this place." Paragraph 756 compares the church building to the New Jerusalem.

There is no mention of a dining room or a dining room table.

LDC's statement: During the celebration of the Eucharist we are "called to the table." The story we celebrate takes flesh upon this table from which we are fed and satisfied.

Response: Although we are certainly "called to the table"—"the altar, around which the Church is gathered in the celebration of the Eucharist, represents the two aspects of the same mystery: the altar of sacrifice and the table of the Lord"[103]—we do not celebrate a "story," we celebrate a sacrament. "The other sacraments, and indeed all ecclesiastical ministries and works of the apostolate, are bound up in the Eucharist and are oriented toward it."[104]

The contemporary liturgist is also fond of speaking of the "celebration of *our* story." The idea that we celebrate ourselves is contrary to the Catholic teaching on the Eucharist. The *Catechism* states that we carry out the command of the Lord "by celebrating the memorial of his sacrifice."[105] The Eucharist is also defined as "the memorial of Christ's Passover, the making present and the sacramental offering of his unique sacrifice."[106]

4. The Crucifix

LDC's statement: The crucifix cannot be said to be a traditional furnishing in Catholic churches. The ancient symbol of Christianity is the cross, not the crucifix. Some crosses have that replica of the body of Jesus, but not all of them do. The corpus was not added to crosses until the 12th century.

Response: This statement is at odds with history: The earliest public symbol of Christianity is neither the cross nor the crucifix; it is the *Agnus Dei*—the Lamb of God. Representations of Our Lord nailed to a cross began to appear in Christian works of art in the 5th century, after Christianity emerged from the catacombs and became a "public" religion. When Christianity was a persecuted religion, prior to the conversion of Constantine (A.D. 312), when crucifixion was still used as a common means of capital pun-

---

[103] *Catechism of the Catholic Church*, 1994, no. 1383.
[104] Ibid., no. 1324.
[105] Ibid., no. 1357.
[106] Ibid., no. 1362.

ishment, Christians did not use the crucifix as an icon. It was simply too conspicuous.

The Council of Constantinople in A.D. 629 ordered: "That, instead of the lamb, our Lord Jesus Christ will be shown hereafter in His human form in images so that we shall be led to remember His mortal life, His passion, and His death, which paid the ransom for mankind." This image was the crucifix.

As the Church developed in its devotional piety and customs, the crucifix came to be recognized as the universal symbol of Christianity. Reformation Protestants in the 16th century, however, rebelled against the use of the crucifix, abandoned the true Church, stripped the corpus from the cross, and splintered off into their own factions, each with their own theologies. Thus, the crucifix came to be identified specifically with the Catholic Church, the bare cross with the "Reformers." As late as 1947, Pope Pius XII was even moved to write that "one would be straying from the straight path were he to... order the crucifix so designed that the divine Redeemer's body shows no trace of His cruel sufferings."[107]

LDC's statement: Reformers rightly removed the corpus from the cross and left Protestants with an instrument of torture. But the Latin cross (✝) is an inadequate symbol for use in our churches today as a symbol for resurrection. Would an electric chair symbolize resurrection? Would we accept the electric chair as a proper symbol of the Christian faith if Jesus had been executed in this century? Instead of using the Latin cross, we ought to use the Greek cross because this form is obscure enough not to be identified with the sacrificial cross, an instrument of torture.

Response: Far from being an inadequate symbol for use in Catholic churches, the crucifix is the *most appropriate* and fullest symbolic expression of the Christian faith. The tra-

---

[107] Pope Pius XII, *Mediator Dei*, 1947, no. 62.

dition of the Church includes many different types of crucifixes. For the past several hundred years the most common was the cross with Jesus' wounded body hanging from the wood. [108]

No Church document so much as hints that this form of the crucifix is inappropriate. It is simply a subjective and contrived opinion of the archi-liturgical establishment that a preference be given to the cross (whether the Latin or Greek form is promoted) without a corpus. The *General Instruction of the Roman Missal* speaks little about the placement or design of crucifixes. It simply states that there is to be "a cross, clearly visible to the congregation, either on the altar or near it." [109] But since the Mass is inseparably connected to the Crucifixion (not the Resurrection), the crucifix, a representation of the Lord's Body upon the Cross, directly symbolizes the whole meaning of the Mass. Pope Pius XII explains:

> The august sacrifice of the altar is [...] no mere simple commemoration of the Passion and Death of Jesus Christ; it is truly and properly the offering of a sacrifice, wherein by an unbloody immolation the High Priest does what He has already done on the Cross, offering Himself to the eternal Father as a most acceptable victim. "One... and the same is the victim, one and the same is He who now offers by the ministry of His priests and who then offered Himself on the Cross; the difference is only in the manner of offering." [110]

The objection to using the shape of the Latin cross reveals that the LDC does not believe the sacrificial nature of

---

[108] Most modern "Resurrection Crosses" show our Lord's body detached from the cross, thus not expressing the important reality of the Crucifixion.

[109] *General Instruction of the Roman Missal*, Fourth edition, 1975, no. 270.

[110] Pope Pius XII, *Mediator Dei*, 1947, no. 68. Cf. Council of Trent, Canons and Decrees, no. 145-46.

the Mass should be considered. However, since the crucifix, directly symbolizes the meaning of the Mass, it calls to mind the various facets of the Lord's act of sacrifice—"becoming man and taking the form of a slave (cf. Phil 2:7), taking away the sins of the world (cf. Jn 1:29), his Passion and Death—and further serves to remind the faithful of their obligation to share in Christ's sufferings. It also calls to mind the Resurrection."[111] Given these understandings, the connection between the crucifix and the Mass cannot be overstated. A Greek, plus-sign-shape cross (✚) is simply unable to make this connection between the Crucifixion and the Mass. Nor is it a particularly suitable or useful symbol for the Resurrection.

LDC's statement: No church, when it is renovated, may have a duplication of symbols. Therefore, since only one cross is permitted in the main body of the church, the crosses that surmount the Stations of the Cross must be removed.[112]

Response: No Church document mandates, recommends, or even suggests that each church be limited to displaying one Cross. The *Enchiridion*, Handbook of Indulgences, however, calls for 14 crosses on the Stations, one atop each Station. How many souls have been confused, distracted, or led astray by "duplication of symbols" in a church? The

---

[111] Schloeder, Steven J., *Architecture in Communion*, San Francisco: Ignatius Press, 1998, p. 80.

[112] In an open letter from Mary Wilson (September 21, 1999) to her fellow parishioners at St. Francis Xavier Church in Petoskey, Michigan, she related a recent trip she had taken to St. Mary's Church in Alpena, Mich. She writes: "...As we continued our walk I looked up to see the Stations of the Cross. They were shaped square at the bottom but with a point at the top. This point had nothing affixed to it. I immediately said, 'You know, it looks like there may have been crosses at the top of those Stations.' The [business manager] replied, 'Yes, I guess I lost that battle. They were removed and I have them saved in a box.' 'Why were they removed?' I asked. He said, 'because you can't have duplicating symbols.'"

LDC's statement is simply another ripe example of a sub-jective and contrived opinion being used to justify reduc-tionism in church architecture.

5. The Use of Statuary and Shrines

LDC's statement: The presence of statues in the sanctuary cause parishioners to be confused about the difference between devotion to the saints and the celebration of the Eucharist.

Response: Take a survey, or just use common sense. How many people do you know who are confused about the difference between devotion to the saints and the celebra-tion of the Eucharist? Statuary and other works of sacred art are meant to complement the central focus of public worship, the Eucharist. Sacred art is to draw us in visually to focus on the Mass at the altar of sacrifice.

Sacrosanctum Concilium, the Constitution on the Sacred Liturgy reminds us that the sacrifice of the Mass takes place in the presence of the angels and saints. Their repre-sentation in a church is a physical representation of that relationship, and their place in the Church Triumphant:

"In the earthly liturgy we take part in a foretaste of that heavenly liturgy which is celebrated in the holy city of Jerusalem toward which we journey as pilgrims, where Christ is sitting at the right hand of God, a minister of the holies and of the true tabernacle; we sing a hymn to the Lord's glory with all the warriors of the heavenly army; venerating the memory of the saints, we hope for some part and fellowship with them; we eagerly await the Savior, Our Lord Jesus Christ, until He, our life, shall appear and we too will appear with Him in glory." [113]

---

[113] Pope Paul VI, *Sacrosanctum Concilium*, 1963, no. 8.

LDC's statement: *The "noble simplicity" called for by the Council's Constitution on the Sacred Liturgy (Sacrosanctum Concilium) means that we cannot keep statues of the saints in the church. Statues will distract our attention from the main focus, which is the celebration of the Eucharist.*

Response: The Second Vatican Council's *Constitution on the Sacred Liturgy* states that the "practice of placing sacred images in churches so that they may be venerated by the faithful is to be maintained. Nevertheless their number should be moderate and their relative positions should reflect right order."[114]

"Noble simplicity" refers to the rites of the Church, not its furnishings or architecture. According to paragraph 34 of *Sacrosanctum Concilium,* "the rites should be distinguished by noble simplicity."[115] Sacred furnishings, such as statuary, should reflect "noble beauty": "Ordinaries, by the encouragement and favor they show to art which is truly sacred, should strive after noble beauty rather than mere extravagance."[116]

Further, *Opera Artis,* issued by the Vatican in 1971 states that "Works of art from the past are always and everywhere to be preserved so that they may lend their noble service to divine worship and their help to the people's active participation in the liturgy."[117] *Sacrosanctum Concilium* said the same thing in 1963: "Ordinaries should ensure that sacred furnishings and works of value are not disposed of or destroyed, for they are ornaments in God's house."[118]

Throughout the history of the Church, saints have always had their place in the church building. These icons, whether painting, sculptures or bas-reliefs, are meant to

---

[114] Ibid., no. 125.
[115] Ibid., no. 34.
[116] Ibid., no. 124.
[117] Sacred Congregation for the Clergy, *Opera Artis,* 1971.
[118] Pope Paul VI, *Sacrosanctum Concilium,* 1963, no. 126.

give physical expression to the passage from St. Paul's Epistle to the Hebrews: "We are surrounded by so great a cloud of witnesses" (Heb 12:1).

In 1947 Pope Pius XII warned: "It would be wrong, for example... [if] pictures and statues were excluded from our churches."[119]

LDC's statement: Shrines (side altars) came about as a medieval introduction due to indulgences. The laity paid for Masses to be said for the dead, believing that the celebration of Mass would deliver them from purgatory. The shrine in the church is an outdated and defunct artifact. It has no place in contemporary church architecture.

Response: Although many LDCs today take pleasure in denigrating the Church's doctrine of Purgatory, it is nonetheless an unalterable defined doctrine of the Church. The shrine is certainly not outdated or defunct. Nor is it an artifact. It remains a living part of the Church's rich artistic heritage.

In September, 1999, the Vatican released a new edition of the Enchiridion of Indulgences, which outlines the current guidelines for indulgences. At a press conference Cardinal William Wakefield Baum offered the following comments: "Catholic doctrine on indulgences is based on very precise theological assumptions and on well-documented historical precedents of Tradition." Father Ivan Fucek, assistant theologian of the Apostolic Penitentiary [which published the Vatican guidelines] said the Church's doctrine on indulgences and Purgatory, which is denied by some, is clearly expressed in St. Thomas [Aquinas]. But he was not the one who 'invented' it; it was implicit in the Church's doctrine from the very beginning. The Councils that followed merely confirmed it."[120]

---

[119] Pope Pius XII, *Mediator Dei*, 1947, no. 66, 201.
[120] Zenit News Service, Sept. 17, 1999.

LDC's statement: Each church may have only one image of any saint. So if, for instance, you have two statues of Mary. You will have to make a choice. Which one do you want to stay?

Response: Architect Steven J. Schloeder addresses this issue well in his 1998 book *Architecture in Communion: Implementing the Second Vatican Council through Liturgy and Architecture:*

"The *General Instruction [of the Roman Missal...* states: 'There is need...to limit their number... There is to be only one image of any saint.' 'Limit their number' is also a rather subjective guideline, which the Church recognizes by qualifying, 'In general, the devotion of the entire community is to be the criterion regarding images in the adornment and arrangement of a church.'[121] The injunction against more than one image of a particular saint is meant, I think, to address the use of statues in veneration shrines, rather than to be an outright forbidding of replication. That is to say, it does not seem that to have a titular representation of Saint John the Baptist in an apsidal mosaic, a painted icon depicting the Baptism of Christ in the baptistery, a place of veneration with a titular statue of the Baptist, and perhaps even another stained-glass portrait would violate the intention of the rule. The point of the injunction is to have only one place of veneration, typically with votive candles, for any particular saint.

The injunction does not apply to crucifixes and multiple images of our Lord, or even our Lady insofar as she appears under her various titles. Were this the case, both St. Peter's in Rome and the Shrine of the Immaculate Conception in Washington, D.C., would have to undergo thorough overhauls.[122]

---

[121] *General Instruction of the Roman Missal,* fourth edition, 1975, no. 278.
[122] Schloeder, Steven J., *Architecture in Communion,* San Francisco: Ignatius Press, 1998, p. 153.

LDC's statement: The church should include representations of some of our modern day religious folk heroes, those who will serve as visual reminders of modern-day religious role models who can inspire us to lead lives of holiness.

Response: The sacred image or icon has always been an important part of the Catholic church building. Through works of sacred art, artists and artisans have long depicted the truths of the Gospel in material media. Statues, painted icons, frescoes, mosaics and stained glass, according to Catholic tradition, help us to focus prayer and meditation. These images also instruct us in the truths of the faith by depicting Jesus, the Holy Trinity, the Blessed Mother, the angels and the saints.

Choosing to depict images that are not in the tradition of the Church can be criticized on a number of grounds. The most important reason is that the selection of "non-saints" subverts the Church's process of canonization. Depicting contemporary role models or "religious folk heroes" — Catholic or not — however, further undermines the artistic tradition and theology of the sacred icon by providing instead a "profane" icon.

According to the Second Vatican Council, "Those decrees, which were given in the early days regarding the cult images of Christ, the Blessed Virgin and the saints [are to] be religiously observed."[123] In choosing to depict the profane, the consultant aligns himself with the ancient "iconoclasts" who broke with the authentic tradition of the Church by forbidding representations of Christ and religious images in general. Pope John Paul II explains in his 1987 apostolic letter *Duodecimum saeculum,* and again in his 1999 "Letter to Artists," that the iconoclasts, "not without contradiction or ambiguity, continued to allow profane im-

---

[123] Vatican II, *Lumen Gentium,* 1964, no. 67.

ages, in particular those of the Emperor, with the signs of reverence that were attached to them."[124]

In his book *Architecture in Communion*, architect Steven J. Schloeder explains that "in mystical theology an icon is a sacred image that is a sort of window to another level of understanding, through which one contemplates a spiritual reality." We were created, writes Schloeder, "to respond to religious art so that our hearts could be moved by the portrayal of beauty and truth."[125]

Catholics do this properly through veneration. In the words of the *Catechism of the Catholic Church*, by way of St. Thomas Aquinas, "the honor rendered to an image passes to its prototype,"[126] and "whoever venerates an image venerates the person portrayed in it."[127] Thus if the profane icon is venerated, the non-saint himself is venerated. This presents a number of problems, and is indicative of a distorted understanding of the communion of saints, which might be more accurately dubbed the "communion of role models," or even a sort of "anti-communion of the saints."[128]

Pope John Paul II has canonized more saints than any previous pope, including many "contemporary role models." Thus, there exists an ample pool of saintly candidates who have gone through the rigorous process of scrutiny by the Church and have been formally declared "worthy of veneration by the faithful."

---

[124] John Paul II, *Duodecimum saeculum*, 1987, no. 8

[125] Schloeder, Steven J., *Architecture in Communion: Implementing the Second Vatican Council through Liturgy and Architecture*, San Francisco: Ignatius Press, 1998, page 148.

[126] *Catechism of the Catholic Church*, 1994, no. 2129.

[127] Ibid., no. 2132.

[128] Popular non-saints who have been memorialized in recent Catholic church projects include Martin Luther King, Gandhi, Dr. Tom Dooley, Oscar Romero, and Cardinal Joseph Bernardin.

6. The Baptismal Font/Baptistery

LDC's statement: Immersion is the *"norm"* (or *"preferred method"*) for baptism in the church today.

Response: Church documents lend no support to this statement. Church guidelines state that a baptistery "must be reserved for the sacrament of baptism and should be entirely worthy, as befits the place where Christians are reborn from water and the Holy Spirit."[129] The baptistery is to be a clearly defined space apart from the sanctuary, where it should be "capable of accommodating a large number of people" and in a prominent place where it is clearly visible."[130]

LDC's statement: Although during the 1970's and 80's, liturgists typically placed the font in or near the sanctuary, the baptismal font really should be located at the entrance to the "worship space."

Response: In this particular instance the design consultant or liturgist is admitting that the preferred fashion they chose to implement in the 1970's was not the proper solution. If the archi-liturgical establishment was wrong once regarding placement and design of the baptismal font, why should we now believe that the current fad is the right one? They certainly cannot appeal to church documents, alleging that this is somehow mandatory. That would be admitting that they had once been disregarding the mandates of Church authorities.

In Toledo, Ohio's cathedral, the baptismal font, a beautiful work of art, was switched with the tabernacle. In a previous renovation project the baptismal font was moved

---

[129] Sacred Congregation for Worship, *Per initiationis Christianae*, 1973, no. 25.
[130] Ibid.

behind the altar of sacrifice and the tabernacle, another beautiful work of art, was moved into the baptistery. In other words, what was once the chapel for baptism is now the Blessed Sacrament chapel. Because the baptistery was not designed to accommodate Eucharistic devotion it is unable to do so. The former baptistery, because of its size and shape, actually fights against any devotion. The stained glass window in the baptistery features the baptism of Christ by John the Baptist. Quite a lot of symbolism is lost because of the inappropriateness of the tabernacle being located in the baptistery. At the same time the new position of the baptismal font—it is not an immersion pool—behind the altar is, at best, strange.

LDC's statement: *Holy water fonts (or "stoops") should not be used. The baptismal font ought to be used for blessing oneself upon entering the church. The water ought to be "living water"; therefore the water should bubble or cascade in the baptismal font.*

Response: Holy water fonts ("stoops") are an extension of the baptismal pool, and if similar in design, can reinforce this fact. The practice of "bubbling and cascading" is the product of modern advances in plumbing, and as such is not inspired by the early Church.

There is no document which discourages the use of fonts.

One of main problems with the design of modern immersion baptismal pools, especially when they have bubbling water, is that they bear a remarkable resemblance to hot tubs and jacuzzis. Another problem is that the bubbling, cascading, or flowing water can be a real distraction during the Mass. Liturgists are adamant about the tabernacle, statues, murals, icons and shrines not distracting anyone from the liturgy. The sound of bubbling water is very annoying to many people. It has also been said that the sound of running water makes one's bladder become more active than is desirable during Mass.

7. Communion Rails

LDC's statement: In 1969 (or 1970, etc.) the Vatican instructed that communion rails should be removed from all churches. They present an unnecessary barrier between the priest and the people. Some pastors, however, in defiance of the Church have neglected to remove their communion rails.

Response: Nowhere in Church documents is it even suggested that the communion rail must be removed or that it cannot be in the plans of a new church. Article 258 of the *General Instruction of the Roman Missal* states that the "sanctuary should be marked off from the nave by a higher floor level or by a distinctive structure and décor."[131]

It would seem that the communion rail would properly qualify as a "distinctive structure" that could be used to mark off the sanctuary from the nave, especially given that it has been used universally since the 16th century, and much earlier in some places.

Father John Trigilio has this to say on the subject:

"There is no official document from Rome which ever mandated or even suggested that altar railings be removed or not installed when building new churches. Vatican II and subsequent legislation merely give the option to receive Holy Communion in the hand (if the bishop permits) or on the tongue. Communion may be given while kneeling or standing... How and why communion rails got removed is a curious phenomenon. It just happened and no one asked why. Neither the Vatican nor the NCCB mandated it yet the liturgical "experts" forced it upon us as if it were law. As to the docu-

---

[131] *General Instruction of the Roman Missal*, 1973, no. 258.

mentation to allow Communion railings, Roman law has a principle that if it [a thing] is not forbidden, it is permitted *especially* if it was done in the past."[132]

LDC's statement: *The communion rail was a medieval addition to the church building based on erroneous theology. Its main purpose was to keep the dogs and other rabble out of the sanctuary.*

Response: The use of some sort of architectural "barrier" to separate the nave from the sanctuary dates from at least the 4th century. Oupensky states that there exists some archeological evidence of earlier chapels in the catacombs arranged with a low railing separating the nave from the apse.[133]

The precursor to the communion rail, or altar rail, is the *cancelli* (also called *septum* or *transenna*). This was a balustraded wall which protected the altar from irreverences. In the Byzantine church the barrier took the form of the iconostasis, an elaborate screen decorated with icons and pierced by three doors. Various other forms of "distinctive structure" were used to mark off the sanctuary from the nave before it universally evolved into the communion rail of the 16th-20th centuries.

The communion rail merely emphasizes the hierarchic separation that is found throughout the Church and across the ages. Bishop Guillaume Durand taught in his 1843 treatise *Rationale Divinorum Officiorum* that the communion rail "teaches the separation of things celestial from things terrestrial."

More than a century later (but before communion rails were unceremoniously removed from thousands of Catholic churches in the name of liturgical innovation), Father J. O'Connell explained one of the many theological reasons

---

[132] Triligilio, EWTN Website, (http://www.ewtn.com) March 30, 1999.
[133] Oupensky, L., *The Theology of the Icon*, Crestwood NY: St. Vladimir's Seminary Press, 1978, page 87.

behind the use of the rail: "Although lay folk normally receive Holy Communion at the Communion rail, they are supposed to be receiving the Body of Christ *from* the altar of sacrifice, and so it is preferable to think of the Communion rail rather as a prolongation of the altar... Hence the ideal is to construct the rail to resemble somewhat the altar (the same material, style, decoration, etc.)."[134]

Kneeling to receive holy Communion is still the preferred method. Pope John Paul II's *Eucharisticum Mysterium* states: "When the faithful communicate kneeling, no other sign of reverence toward the Blessed Sacrament is required, since kneeling is itself a sign of adoration.

Architect Steven J. Schloeder writes, "Since the Church suggests that the faithful revere the Eucharist by communicating in this posture [kneeling], it seems inadvisable to remove the opportunity for doing so. There is also a dimension of community provided by kneeling together to receive Communion...side by side in a silent profession of faith."[135]

8. Pews or chairs?

LDC's statement: Pews with kneelers are not a part of our Catholic heritage. Pews are an American (or Scottish Presbyterian, or Puritan, etc.) invention.

Response: Americans did not "invent" the church pew. Pews have been an integral part of the Catholic church design since the late Middle Ages. From the 13th century, some churches already had backless benches. Pews, as we think of them today, were used by both the Protestant "re-

---

[134] O'Connell, Fr. J., *Church Building and Furnishing, the Church's Way*, London: Burns and Oates, 1955, page 13.
[135] Schloeder, Steven J., *Architecture in Communion*, San Francisco: Ignatius Press, 1998, page 79.

formers" and the Catholics of the Counter-Reformation. This reflected a new emphasis on the proclamation of the Word and preaching.

By the late 16th century most Catholic churches being built included wooden pews with kneelers and high backs. Those churches that did not have pews had kneeling benches called *predelle*.

Pews are always and everywhere acceptable. They are not, however, required. It is interesting to note that the unity candle came from the Protestant tradition and many of the currently pop Masses and songs sung in Catholic parishes are of decidedly Protestant origin. Yet modern liturgists would not be willing to throw these away based on the claim that they are "not part of Catholic heritage."

Yet regardless of who started the practice of using wooden pews, it has become an important part of the Catholic heritage in the Americas. Liturgists prefer to use interlocking chairs for numerous (often dubious) reasons. One repercussion of favoring chairs over pews is that the kneeler is lost. Thus, the act of kneeling in worship is also lost.

It might be said too that chairs for seating are certainly not a part of Catholic tradition. Before pews were used churches made no provision for sitting and kneeling. The faithful either stood and kneeled on the stone floor or they brought their own cushions to kneel upon.

LDC's statement: *If you go to a church in Europe you will notice that almost all the churches there have moveable chairs, not wooden pews with kneelers.*

Response: Again, when most Americans visit Europe they tend to visit the large basilicas and cathedrals that are of great historical and artistic significance. These tend to be large churches that attract a fair amount of tourist traffic each day. They were designed to accommodate large congregations for the celebration of Mass; thus many, such as the Gothic cathedrals of France and Germany have never had pews.

It is preposterous however to apply that to all the churches in Europe. In fact, most churches have indeed had pews with kneelers, at least since the 16th century. Pick up any of the numerous coffee table books that feature Catholic church architecture from Europe. One will notice consistently the use of traditional pews.

LDC's statement: Moveable chairs are preferable because we are a "pilgrim people," always on the move. Moveable chairs allow for flexible arrangements to accommodate the various rites of the Church (e.g. Mass of Christian burial, weddings, baptisms, etc.)

Response: Liturgists and design consultants have been indoctrinated to promote the popular archi-liturgical concept of "flexibility." The various designs used to promote flexibility are really ways to completely redefine the whole Catholic church building, doing so on the model of a secular or profane building, one that is not set aside for sacred purposes.

The dominant culture may be fleeting and in constant flux with no absolutes, yet the Church stands as a timeless witness to the history and salvation of man (the pilgrim people), unchanging in its essentials, but diverse in its nonessentials. It does not stand to reason that since we are a "pilgrim people" we ought *not* to have stable environments in which to worship. Rather we as a pilgrim people ought to be fed through the stable environment of the Church and Catholic culture. This ought necessarily be reflected in the church building. According to *Lumen Gentium*, the Second Vatican Council's constitution on the Church (and reiterated in the *Catechism of the Catholic Church*, paragraph 756):

"The Church has often been called the edifice of God (1 Cor 3:9). Even the Lord likened Himself to the stone which the builders rejected, but which became the cornerstone (Mt 21:42, Acts 4:11, 1 Pet 2:7, Ps 117:22). On this foundation the Church is built by the apostles (1 Cor 3:11), and from it the Church receives durability and solidity. This edifice is adorned by various names: the house of God (1 Tm 3:15) in which dwells His family; the household of God in the Spirit (Eph 2:19-22), the dwelling place of God among men (Apoc 21:3), and especially, the holy temple. This temple, symbolized by places of worship built out of stone, is praised by the holy Fathers and, not without reason, is compared in the liturgy to the Holy City, the New Jerusalem. As living stones we here on earth are being built up along with this City."[136]

LDC's statement: Kneeling[137] *is not a posture of "celebration." Since the liturgy is celebrated, there is no longer any need for kneeling during the liturgy.*

Response: This statement contradicts the GIRM—"[the people] should kneel at the consecration"[138]—and the U.S. appendix comment on this article. Saying that the liturgy is "celebrated" is true, but this is not a celebration akin to a New Year's Eve party. As with most words in the English language, "celebrate" has a number of different meanings

---

[136] Pope Paul VI, *Lumen Gentium*, 1964, no. 6.
[137] "Parishioners are also bothered that [LDC Christine] Reinhard's presentations are systematically critical of piety, holiness, sacredness and traditions of the Catholic faith. She ridiculed, for instance, the posture of kneeling, which she sees merely as a 'penitential pose' that is not proper for the enlightened Catholics of today's America. Reinhard told parishioners that kneeling originated with the medieval peasants who bowed to their masters. They would kneel down, she said, and expose the nape of their necks in case the lord wanted to chop off their heads" (*The Wanderer*, Sept. 9, 1999).
[138] *General Instruction of the Roman Missal*, 1973, no. 21.

(senses). The primary meaning of celebrate, according to *Webster's New World Dictionary*, is "to perform (a ritual, ceremony, etc.) publicly and formally; solemnize." Its second sense is "to commemorate with ceremony." It is in these two senses that the celebration of the Mass has its meaning. Jesus did say "do this in memory of me."

Next we must realize that celebration of the liturgy includes many different parts with different aspects, e.g., praise, penance, adoration, etc. To ignore these different aspects of the celebration is to summarily dismiss it. The richness and meaning of the Holy Sacrifice of the Mass would be lost.

To say that kneeling is not a posture of celebration would only be true if one were speaking of celebration in the sense of a party or festivity, which the Holy Mass, (whether or not the archi-liturgical establishment concurs) is not.

LDC's statement: *Pews are not required by any liturgical document. In fact, they have never been required.*

Response: This statement, however true, cannot justify the removal of pews from an existing church. No liturgical document of the Church requires any specific type of seating, including portable chairs. The use of pews in Catholic church architecture is customary. Canon 27 states, "Custom is the best interpreter of laws."

9. The shape and arrangement of a church

LDC's statement: *The fan-shaped, amphitheater arrangement encourages active participation in the Mass.*

Response: The amphitheater was popular in the Pagan days of Greece and Rome. The early Church was well familiar with it. Yet churches in that shape were first designed in the 19th century by Protestants who built their liturgies around the power of the preacher. This is a fine shape for a theater or a lecture hall, but there is no proof that this arrangement encourages active participation. How much active participation is there from the assembly in the theater or lecture hall?

One of the presumptions of the fan-shaped amphitheater arrangement is that it better allows the entire congregation to "see" the altar and the actions of the liturgy. ("Seeing," incidentally, is a passive experience.) Ironically in contemporary churches such arrangements may bring the furthest pews (or chairs) in the nave closer to the altar, but at the same time the altar is lowered to the same plane as the seating (or just a bit higher). In such an arrangement almost no one can see the altar or the various actions of the liturgy.

As far as that is concerned, in the traditional church arrangement, the sanctuary is elevated, not only to differentiate the space from that of the congregation, but to enable the man in the pew to see the altar and the actions of the liturgy. Likewise the design of the pulpit, which was traditionally elevated with a set of stairs leading to it, enabled the congregation to best see and hear the priest or deacon as he read the gospel and preached the homily.

LDC's statement: Benches or chairs for seating the assembly should be so constructed and arranged that they maximize feelings of community involvement.[139]

Response: This statement reflects a mere sociological understanding of the liturgy. See the next response.

---

[139] Bishops Committee on Liturgy, *Environment and Art in Catholic Worship*, 1978, no. 68.

LDC's statement: The *"in-the-round" arrangement is preferable because then everyone in the congregation is able to feel as if the table belongs equally to the entire community.*

Response: The table (an altar, to be precise) does not belong to the community that is merely assembled in the church. That would be a Congregationalist view of worship, not a Catholic one. The altar of sacrifice belongs to Christ and His Church.

The Church (*Lumen Gentium,* chapter 3), the church building (GIRM, no. 257) and the liturgy (GIRM, no.257) have hierarchies. Trying to make everything "level" or "equal" is contrary to the nature of the Church, the church building, and the Mass.

Lumen Gentium, the Second Vatican Council's Constitution on the Church clearly states that "Taking part in the Eucharistic Sacrifice, which is the fount and apex of the whole Christian life, they offer the divine Victim to God, and offer themselves along with It. Thus, both by the act of oblation and through holy Communion, all perform their proper part in this liturgical service, not, indeed, all in the same way but each in that way which is appropriate to himself."[140]

LDC's statement: When *seats are lined up in rows, all the focus is placed on the people in the front. In this arrangement we really worship the backs of people's heads.*

Response: The statement is stranger than most because the same LDCs who complain about "head-worshipping" are advocating that we gather in a circle so that we may see one another. When we gather in a circle the focus is not placed on the "people in the front," but all the people who form the circle. So positioned we are, according to the consultant's logic, worshipping the faces and full front bodies

---

[140] Pope Paul VI, *Lumen Gentium,* 1964, no. 11.

of those individuals who make up the gathered assembly. But not only that, everyone, save for those who are seated in the innermost concentric circle (i.e., the front row), still worships the back of the heads that are still in front of them.

When seats are lined up in rows, the traditional arrangement, the congregation focuses on what is up front – that is, the liturgical actions of the rite: the Holy Sacrifice, the proclamation of the gospel, etc.

LDC's statement: If you count about eight or nine pews back, that seems to be joined to the altar area, but once you get out further than that you forget what Mass is all about. It's about celebration together. In the round situation we will be celebrating together, joined together, to receive Christ and his blessings.

Response: The GIRM does not call for any particular arrangement of the Church. It simply states: "The people of God assembled at Mass possess an organic and hierarchical structure, expressed by the various ministries and actions for each part of the celebration. The general plan of the sacred edifice should be such that in some way it conveys the image of the gathered assembly. It should also allow the participants to take the place most appropriate to them and assist all to carry out their individual functions properly."[141]

There is still no evidence that the "in-the-round" arrangement provides a better worship environment for celebration together. Nor does it necessarily mean that no one will be sitting further than eight or nine rows from the altar.

LDC's statement: The traditional basilica shape adopted by Constantine is no longer suitable for our new liturgy.

---

[141] *General Instruction of the Roman Missal*, Fifth Edition, 1975, no. 257.

Response: This statement cannot be supported by any Church document throughout the history of the Church. There is no indication in either *Sacrosanctum Concilium* or the GIRM that even suggests that the basilica arrangement is inappropriate or unsuitable to the 1970 Roman rite.

LDC's statement: St. Peter's Basilica in Rome allows for church-in-the-round seating. If it's good enough for the Pope then it ought to be good enough for you.

Response: The Basilica of St. Peter marks the tomb of a martyr, St. Peter, which is traditionally rendered architecturally in a Greek cross format or in a circular shape. A *martyrium* (as this type of building is called) is a different architectural type. There are many fine examples, especially in Italy, of this type of church building. However there is no need to apply this "type" to all church buildings.

If we are to use St. Peter's Basilica as a model to design our parish churches then our churches also ought to include baldachinos, numerous shrines and chapels, rows of statuary, a catacomb, ornate murals, etc.

Contrary to popular belief, St. Peter's Basilica is not the Pope's Cathedral. The cathedral of His Holiness is the Basilica of St. John Lateran in Rome. Interestingly, it is of the traditional basilica arrangement. If it's good enough for the Pope then it's good enough for me!

10. Designing for the Assembly

LDC's statement: The word "church" comes from the Greek "ecclesia," meaning assembly or gathering. Therefore we ought to view our worship space as a gathering room, a place of assembly.

Response: The English word "church" actually comes from the Greek word KYRIAKON, which means "the Lord's house." The Latin word for church, *ecclesia,* also comes from the Greek. EKKLESIA originally denoted a solemnly convoked and organized assembly, especially a political assembly of the sovereign people. EKKLESIA was originally the people called to arms, i.e., the people as militia. Etymologically, the word is derived from EKKALEIN, meaning "to call out, summon." In the Septuagint, the word is applied to the whole people of Israel in solemn convocation. The Greek language is not lacking for words denoting the mere fact of "gathering" or a coming together of individuals into one place for any purpose. "Assembly," like *ecclesia,* connotes a solemn convocation. "Gathering" does not and is a poor translation of *ecclesia.*

Even if *ecclesia* in certain contexts has borne the meaning "assembly of Christians" or even "gathering of Christians," it does not follow that the word in all contexts denotes these things or even that its meaning in a particular context is significantly colored by its etymology. In fact, the normal use of *ecclesia* denotes unambiguously and exclusively the same concepts denoted in English by "church," without any accessory notion of "gathering" or "assembly"

If we don't sever our ties to the past 2000 years of history, we easily understand the necessity of the church building as a place set apart for the worship of God—a sacred, not a profane place. If we were to simply view our place of worship as a "gathering room" or a "place of assembly" we could use the cafeteria, school room, courthouse, theater, or any other place of gathering, as our "worship space."

But churches are built *ad maiorem Dei gloriam,* for the greater glory of God, rather than for the accommodation of a crowd of people. With this in mind *The Rites for the Dedication of a Church* states that "When a church is erected as a building destined solely and permanently for assembling the people of God and for carrying out sacred functions, it is fitting that it be dedicated to God with a solemn rite, in accordance with the ancient custom of the Church."

LDC's statement: The 1978 bishops' document "Environment and Art in Catholic Worship" states that the "norm for designing liturgical space is the assembly and its liturgies. The building or cover enclosing the architectural space is a shelter or 'skin' for a liturgical action."

Response: In the Holy Father's encyclical *Christifidelis Laici*, Pope John Paul II states that church buildings are necessarily representations of the Church.[142] EACW consistently reveals an antagonism toward the church building as a "place." It rather suggests that the church should be a non-place, a multi-purpose assembly hall. Speaking of the building as a "cover," a "shelter," or a "skin" is extremely short-sighted. "This view," writes architect Duncan Stroik in his critique of the 1978 document, "growing out of the American meeting house tradition, parallels the recent success of the megachurch movement in which the building is consciously designed not to look like a church or anything else...

"The document says very little about the exterior of the church, its signification as a '*domus ecclesiae*,' and its appropriate siting in the city or the country. There is no recognition of the scriptural metaphors of the city set on a hill, the lamp on a lampstand or the city of God. The ability of the church building to symbolize the Christian community and her belief in Christ, through domes, spires, bells, generous portals, atriums, gardens, and iconography is ignored."[143]

---

[142] Pope John Paul II, *Christifidelis Laici*, 1988, no.25.
[143] Stroik, Duncan, "Environment and Art in Catholic Worship: A Critique," *Sacred Architecture*, Summer, 1999.

In the limited and unfortunate view of church architecture as outlined in EACW, there is no room for "great buildings for worship, in which the functional is always wedded to the creative impulse inspired by a sense of the beautiful and an intuition of the mystery,"[144] as Pope John Paul II calls for in his 1999 *Letter to Artists*.

In short, never in the history of Catholic church architecture has the church building been reduced to a "skin for a liturgical action." To regard it as such betrays a grave misunderstanding of the Church and her building tradition.

Rather than enveloping a "liturgical space," the church ought to be designed with reference and understanding of the architectural "typology" (i.e., model) of the church building. To do so the architect must know and understand the various types or models that recur throughout Christian history.

Four of the most common types are the basilica, hall, cruciform and centralized plans. Each has its own historical derivation and theological expression. Each of these types has its own principles of axes, symmetry, hierarchy, and volume which must be followed for the building to be integral and coherent.

When a designer understands the church building simply as a "skin for a liturgical action," he is unable to draw upon the rich tradition the Church offers each age. The results are buildings that are not only banal and uninspiring, but they are buildings that are not churches.

LDC's statement: "Flexibility" and "hospitality" are the two main design considerations to accommodate when designing or renovating a "worship space."

Response: Taking "flexibility" and "hospitality" as the two main design considerations reveals the desire to look to-

---

[144] Pope John Paul II, *Letter to Artists*, 1999, no. 8.

ward the so-called "needs of the assembly" (not to be confused with "what the people want") rather than to the needs of the Church.

These two design considerations are mere fads, based on the archi-liturgical theories of the 1960's—theories which are in essence Modernist and anti-Church, specifically anti-Catholic. Traditionally the highest goal of the church building was "transcendence," creating a sense of the other-worldly, the supernatural, the divine—the focus being on God. With transcendence in mind, the Christian artists of the past 2000 years have developed stained-glass windows, ornate domes, rose windows, icons, statues, and so forth.

"Flexibility" and "hospitality" on the other hand reflect a focus on the congregation. These two design considerations are often invoked to justify eliminating pews, removing the elements which define the sanctuary from the nave,

LDC's statement: Our very act of assembly, as well as proclamation of the Word, the service of the liturgical ministers, and the consecrated bread and wine is an experience of the real presence of Christ in our midst.

Response: On its face the statement is true. But one must be attentive to the context in which the statement is made. When the LDC says this the unstated implication normally is: "Christ is just as present in the congregation as in the bread and wine consecrated during the liturgy."

Only the second implied statement, not the explicit first statement, can be used to justify design decisions that will effect moving the tabernacle from the main body of the church as well as rearranging the seating so that the liturgy becomes focused on the group of participants. Yet the second statement is not at all true.

The LDC's statement is based on the explication of the "five presences" of Christ in the liturgy as outlined by Vatican II's *Constitution on the Sacred Liturgy*: "Christ is always present in His Church, especially in her liturgical celebrations. He is present in the sacrifice of the Mass, not only in the person of His minister, 'the same one now offering, through the ministry of priests, who formerly offered himself on the cross,' but *especially under the Eucharistic species*. By His power He is present in the sacraments, so that when a man baptizes it is really Christ Himself who baptizes. He is present in His word, since it is He Himself who speaks when the holy Scriptures are read in the church. He is present, finally, when the Church prays and sings, for He promised: 'Where two or three are gathered together for my sake, there I am in the midst of them (Mt. 18:20).'"[145]

The *Catechism of the Catholic Church* reiterates this teaching in paragraph 1373. The following paragraph, however, delineates the uniqueness of Christ's presence under the Eucharistic species: "The mode of Christ's presence under the Eucharistic species is unique. It raises the Eucharist above all the sacraments as the 'perfection of the spiritual life and the end to which all the sacraments tend.' In the most blessed sacrament of the Eucharist 'the body and blood, together with the soul and divinity of our Lord Jesus Christ and, therefore, *the whole Christ is truly, really, and substantially* contained.'

"This presence is called 'real'—by which is not intended to exclude the other types of presence as if they could not be 'real' too, but because it is presence in the fullest sense: that is to say, it is a *substantial* presence by which Christ, God and man, makes himself wholly and entirely present."[146]

LDC's statement: The assembly itself is the primary symbol of Christ's presence.

---

[145] Pope Paul VI, *Sacrosanctum Concilium*, 1963, no. 7.
[146] *Catechism of the Catholic Church*, 1994, no. 1374.

Response: The assembly itself is not the primary symbol of Christ's presence. Christ is really and substantially present under the Eucharistic species (see *Catechism*, paragraph 1374). Beyond this, the four signs of Christ's presence, as addressed in the previous paragraph, are His ministers, the Sacraments administered by his ministers (deacon, priest and bishop), the Word proclaimed, and when "the Church prays and sings."[147]

LDC's statement: The choir should no longer be located in the choir loft. The needs a space in the sanctuary or at the front of the congregation so that we can better understand the choir as part of the assembly.

Response: How many souls are really confused about the choir being a part of the assembly? "Placement of the choir in church architecture is important, [composer Richard] Proulx said. Using the classical model, which he advocates, the organ and choir will both be located on an axis, usually in the rear gallery of the building. 'It is very reinforcing for the organ and the well-trained voices of the choir to lead from above and behind," he said." Thus, for practical and aesthetic reasons, the choir was placed in its traditional location. The LDC is suggesting that the church must sacrifice the quality of the music in the liturgy to accommodate a fad that places the choir at the front of the assembly for vague symbolic reasons.

11. "Liturgical Code"

LDC's statement: There exists a "hierarchy of documents" in the Church. For example, the liturgical books (e.g. GIRM) supersede all other Church documents, even the Code of Canon Law and the new Catechism. Furthermore, no papal document can contra-

---

[147] Pope Paul VI, *Sacrosanctum Concilium*, 1963, no. 7.

dict anything already published in the General Instruction of the Roman Missal (GIRM).

Response: Documents issued by the authority of the Church when contrary to past laws, including those in the GIRM, or specifically meant to replace past laws, do so. Canon 20 states: "A later law abrogates a former law or derogates from it if it expressly states so, if it is directly contrary to it, or if it entirely re-orders the subject matter of the former law."[148]

The Code of Canon Law doesn't normally discuss liturgical matters, but when it does, it abrogates all past laws on the matter. "For the most part the Code does not define the rites which are to be observed in celebrating liturgical actions. For this reason current liturgical norms retain their force unless a given liturgical norm is contrary to the canons of the Code."[149]

LDC's statement: *When a building, such as an old house is restored it must meet all the contemporary building codes. They had to update the wiring, the heating system, etc. That's what happens when you restore a building in a different age. The same is true in the church. When we restore a church building it has to be restored in light of contemporary requirements. The church must not only meet new building codes, such as requirements for handicap accessibility, it must also meet the requirements of "liturgical code." You can't just do pure restoration unless you're turning your church into a museum.*

Response: Msgr. Peter J. Elliot writes of liturgists: "I believe that these men and women are imprisoned in the recent past because they cling to a kind of 'Maoist' mythology of a perpetual or 'ongoing' liturgical revolution. That mythology is derived from a dated commitment to a per-

---

[148] *Code of Canon Law,* 1983, can. 20.
[149] Ibid., can. 2.

manent program of planned changes rather than to organic and natural development. It has not made these people popular within the wider Church, which they do not always understand."[150]

With that said, it is perhaps easier to understand the *modus operandi* of the contemporary liturgist. He has a permanent program of planned changes. He then constructs "liturgical law" or "liturgical code" to suit this planned program. While it can be said that there exists an authentic "liturgical law" it is not codified in any one source at this time. Further the liturgical law deals mostly with what happens and how it happens at various liturgies. Thus, authentic "liturgical law" has precious little to say about "updates" and "restorations" or anything to do with the architecture or particular designs of church buildings.

It is best to understand most statements uttered by the liturgist or liturgical design consultant in the framework of this Maoist mythology of which Msgr. Elliot speaks.

12. Rights and Responsibilities

LDC's statement: *Those who are objecting to renovation plans by withholding their support are only acting in disobedience to their lawful pastor. All parishioners have an obligation to contribute financially to the needs of the parish.*

Response: If a parishioner is comfortable with the planned renovation he has every right to support it. If he is not pleased with the proposed changes, or believes he has been repeatedly lied to in the process of the renovation project, he has every right to disagree and withhold his financial support. Canon 212 of the Code of Canon Law states: "The Christian faithful are free to make known

---

[150] Elliot, Msgr. Peter J., *Liturgical Question Box*, San Francisco: Ignatius Press, 1998, page 16.

their needs, especially spiritual ones, and their desires to the pastors of the Church... they have the right and even at times the duty to manifest to the sacred pastors their opinion on matters which pertain to the good of the Church, and they have a right to make their opinion known to the other Christian faithful."

Thus, parishioners have the right to disagree with the renovation plans of their church if they believe that these plans would not be for the spiritual good of the parish. The parishioner has the right by law to object by withholding his financial contributions.

LDC's statement: In the Code of Canon Law, canon 222 states: "The Christian faithful are obliged to assist with the needs of the Church so that the Church has what is necessary for divine worship, for apostolic works, and works of charity and for the decent sustenance of ministries." This canon carries the force of a commandment. To break it is a sin. If you do not support our project and our parish financially, the only conclusion that can be anticipated is that you have willfully ceased to function as parishioners.

Response: Catholics have legal and moral obligation to support the Church with their temporal sacrifices. However, the law only states this principle and does not provide concrete norms by which it should be applied. The parish is the usual means through which we receive the spiritual goods of the Church (cf. Cc. 213 and 515) and, as such, it normally has some claim to our support. However, there are a number of worthy causes in the Church and Catholics are free to use their own judgement in deciding how their contributions will be directed.

If a member of a particular parish chooses not support that parish financially, he does not cease to be a parishioner of that parish. Canon 107 states that "Each person acquires a proper pastor and ordinary through both domicile [place of residence] and quasi-domicile [place of temporary residence]." Canon 518 states, "As a general rule a parish is to be territorial, that is it embraces all the Christian faithful within a certain territory.

Thus, registration in a parish, use of the envelope system and the completion of questionnaires are useful and valuable tools to a pastor in his pastoral planning. However, he must respect the rights and provide the spiritual goods of the Church to all who dwell or travel in his parish. Certainly, he may not refuse the sacraments to anyone who legitimately requests them. Anyone who is refused the spiritual goods of the Church solely because he has not contributed a specific amount or his contributions appear to have declined should contact the vicar forane. If a pastor is losing contributions then he needs to ask why.

LDC's statement: A group of disobedient parishioners has decided to hold meetings outside of the renovation process. This is completely out of order. Since the pastor did not approve of this group you should not attend their meetings.[151]

Response: Parishioners are not being disobedient to lawful Church authority by organizing to protect their church from needless renovation changes. In fact, parishioners may justly believe that they not only have the right to do this but also the duty. Canon 212 of the Code of Canon Law states: "The Christian faithful are free to make known their needs, especially spiritual ones, and their desires to the pastors of the Church... they have the right and even

---

[151] When Joe Hoffman, a parishioner at St. Francis Xavier Church in Petoskey, Michigan, invited his pastor to attend an "open forum" sponsored by a group in the parish that formally opposed the renovation process at their church, his pastor responded by calling the forum "cowardly" and "fictitious." He wrote to Hoffman: "Whoever called this meeting is completely out of order... Expect no cooperation from me when things are done behind my back. That type of action is truly cowardly behavior. And no one has authorized you or any other [parishioner] to call this meeting."

at times the duty to manifest to the sacred pastors their opinion on matters which pertain to the good of the Church, and they have a right to make their opinion known to the other Christian faithful."

Actual disobedience must be distinguished from simple disagreement. Disobedience is the intentional disregard or violation of the acts of one who has legitimate authority in the areas in question. Canon 212 instructs that we are obliged to obey even though we may personally believe the act to be inopportune, ill advised, inconvenient, mere folly or even repugnant. For example, if a bishop closes a parish church and reassigns its pastor to another parish, yet the pastor remains at the closed parish and continues to offer the sacraments to parishioners there, the both the pastor and parishioners would be engaging in acts of disobedience.

Disagreement, or the expression of an opinion contrary to an opinion expressed or an act of discretionary judgement by one who holds ecclesiastical office, is permissible, according to Canon 212. We can and may be obliged to disagree with ecclesiastical authorities, as canon 212.3 recognizes, providing that we do so charitably and with due respect for their offices.

13. Miscellaneous Gambits

LDC's statement: I have tried to address your concerns with solid Catholic theology, but it is clear that you are not really interested in the theology of Vatican II. The recommendations I have given were met with hostility and fear because of a lack of understanding about who we are as Catholics.

Response: The LDC has probably not been addressing the parishioners' concerns with "solid Catholic theology." Rather he has likely been repeatedly offering his subjective and contrived opinions and trying to pass them off as the authoritative mandates of Vatican II.

LDC's statement: *As it is clearly set forth in the Code of Canon Law number 846, everyone, including yourself, is to faithfully observe those principles set forth in the liturgical books approved by competent authority. It may not be what you personally like, but the documents and principles stand regardless of one's personal feelings.*

Response: Canon 846 says: "The liturgical books approved by the competent authority are to be faithfully observed in the celebration of the sacraments; therefore no one on personal authority may add, remove or change anything in them." Thus the LDC is correct when he says that everyone is to faithfully observe the principles set forth in the liturgical books approved by the competent authority. But Canon 846 also states that no one may add or change anything in them. This is exactly what liturgical design consultants are doing when they pressure parishioners into accepting radical changes to their church building that are not based on what is set forth in the approved liturgical books, such as the GIRM. The LDCs have long been adding their own subjective and contrived opinions and passing them off as an accepted and approved part of the guidelines set forth in authoritative liturgical documents.

LDC's statement: *It's been 35 years since the Council called us to renew our approach to liturgy. Many parishes did this a long time ago. Yours did not—for whatever reason. If you've been paying attention to anything that's gone on in the Church in the past 35 years you would know that your church is out of date.*

Response: Many parishioners have been paying attention to what has gone on in the Church in the past 35 years. Consequently, they are the ones who understand that many churches have been needlessly destroyed and altered—a financial, artistic, historical and devotional scandal. Although the Council, in *Sacrosanctum Concilium*, did call for Catholics to renew our approach to the liturgy, there is no evidence that the way the so-called renewal was carried out is either in accord with what the Council fathers envisioned or that it was properly translated into the realm of liturgical art and architecture.

LDC's statement: *At any point that a parish has decided to respond to what the Pope asked for, there are going to be people who say, "Well, I'm old now and you're springing this on me." If we had introduced this renovation thirty years ago that generation would have said, "I'm old. Wait until I die, then renovate." The old folks don't die off; they just get replaced.*

Response: It should be clear that it is not just the "old folks" who protest church renovations. This fallacy is based on bigotry and intolerance of the elderly.

LDC's statement: *There is no reason to get so upset or excited. No decisions have been made yet.*

Response: The LDC makes this comment whenever parishioners voice strong objections to the false claims made during the educational sessions. These parishioners, however, are able to understand that the consultant is setting the stage for specific design changes. It may be true that formal decisions (meaning design features) have not been declared, but that does not mean that they have not been made. The renovation process is based on the aggressive marketing of a preset plan that the parish is to choose. Alert parishioners will recognize these techniques early in the process. That is when they should begin to object and inform other parishioners of the preordained product. Countless churches have already been renovated. There are obviously many precedents upon which to draw the conclusion that the basics of the renovation plan have already been set in stone.

CHAPTER 5

Helpful Notes and Quotes
Church Teaching on Liturgical Art & Architecture

෨෬

HIS CHAPTER IS DIVIDED into two sections. The first provides straightforward quotes from various Church documents on such subjects as placement of the tabernacle, definition of a church building, remodeling of churches, church art, worship of the Eucharist, and rights and obligations of the laity. Quotes are taken from authoritative sources such as the *Catechism, Code of Canon Law, General Instruction of the Roman Missal*, papal encyclicals and apostolic exhortations. The second section provides other useful notes and quotes from various personalities in the Church: bishops, priest and laymen.

SECTION 1
Authoritative Church Teaching

The Tabernacle

The tabernacle is to be situated 'in churches in a most worthy place with the greatest honor' (Paul VI, *Mysterium Fidei* 1965); The dignity, placing, and security of the Eu-

charistic tabernacle should foster adoration before the Lord really present in the Blessed Sacrament of the altar.
—*Catechism of the Catholic Church,* 1994, no. 1183

The tabernacle was first intended for the reservation of the Eucharist in a worthy place so that it could be brought to the sick and those absent, outside of Mass. As faith in the Real Presence of Christ in His Eucharist deepened, the Church became conscious of the meaning of silent adoration of the Lord present under the Eucharistic species. It is for this reason that the tabernacle should be located in an especially worthy place in the church and should be constructed in such a way that it emphasizes and manifests the truth of the Real Presence of Christ in the Blessed Sacrament.
—*Catechism of the Catholic Church,* 1994, no.1379

The tabernacle in which the Most Holy Eucharist is reserved should be placed in a part of the church that is prominent, conspicuous, beautifully decorated, and suitable for private prayer.
—*Code of Canon Law,* 1983, can. 938 §2

The Blessed Sacrament is to be reserved in a solid, burglar-proof tabernacle in the center of the high altar if this is really outstanding and distinguished.
—*Inter Oecumeni,*
Sacred Congregation for Rites, 1964, no. 95

The tabernacle in which the Eucharist is kept can be located on an altar, or away from it, in a spot in the church which is very prominent, truly noble, and duly decorated.
—*Inaestimabile Donum,* Pope John Paul II, 1980

"It is highly recommended that the holy eucharist should be reserved in a chapel suitable for private adora-

tion and prayer. If this is impossible because of the structure of the church or local custom, it should be kept on an altar or other place in the church that is prominently and properly decorated." *(reference is then given to Eucharisticum Mysterium, no. 54, see quote below)*
—*General Instruction of the Roman Missal,* 1973, no. 276

The Blessed Sacrament should be reserved in a solid, inviolable tabernacle in the middle of the altar, or in a side altar, but in a truly prominent place.
—*Eucharisticum Mysterium,* Pope Paul VI, 1965, no. 54

The Blessed Sacrament is to be reserved in a solid, burglar-proof tabernacle in the center of the high altar or on another altar if this is really outstanding and distinguished. Where there is lawful custom, and in particular cases to be approved by the local Ordinary, the Blessed Sacrament may be reserved in some other place in the church, but it must be a very special place, having nobility about it, and it must be suitably decorated.
—*Inter Oecumenici,* 1964, no. 95

Note: the following two quotations are not from sources of official Church teaching. They do, however, make clear how both Eucharisticum Mysterium and the GIRM were understood.

The present law, however, directs that the Blessed Sacrament "be reserved in a solid and inviolable tabernacle placed in the middle of the main altar, or on a side altar."
—*The New Catholic Encyclopedia,* 1967

According to directives of the Holy See, since the Second Vatican Council, tabernacles are always solid and inviolable and located in the middle of the main altar or a side altar, but always in a truly prominent place.
—*Catholic Dictionary,* 1979

Definition of a church (building)

The term church signifies a sacred building destined for divine worship to which the faithful have a right of access for divine worship, especially its public exercise.

—*Code of Canon Law,* 1983, can. 1214

When the exercise of religious liberty is not thwarted, Christians construct buildings for divine worship. These visible churches are not simply gathering places but signify and make visible the Church living in this place, the dwelling of God with men reconciled and united in Christ.

A church, a house of prayer in which the Eucharist is celebrated and reserved, where the faithful assemble, and where is worshipped the presence of the Son of God our Savior, offered for us on the sacrificial altar for the help and consolation of the faithful — this house ought to be in good taste and a worthy place for prayer and sacred ceremonial. In this "house of God" the truth and the harmony of the signs that make it up should show Christ to be present and active in this place.

—*Catechism of the Catholic Church,* 1994, no. 1180-81

References to the church building as "the house of God"

All whose concern it is are to take care that such cleanliness and propriety is preserved in churches as befits the house of God and that anything which is out of keeping with the sanctity of the place is precluded.

—*Code of Canon Law,* 1983, can. 1220 §1

Ordinaries [diocesan bishops] must be very careful to see that sacred furnishings and works of value are not disposed of or allowed to deteriorate; for they are the ornaments of the house of God.

—*Sacrosanctum Concilium,* Vatican II, 1963, no. 126

The church, a house of prayer in which the Eucharist is celebrated and reserved, where the faithful assemble, and where is worshipped the presence of the Son of God our Savior, offered for us on the sacrificial altar for the help and consolation of the faithful—this house ought to be in good taste and a worthy place for prayer and sacred ceremonial. In this 'house of God' the truth and harmony of the signs that make it up should show Christ to be present and active in this place.

—*Catechism of the Catholic Church*, 1994, no. 1180-81

Preserving church art and architecture

In the course of the centuries, [the Church] has brought into being a treasury of art which must be very carefully preserved.

—*Sacrosanctum Concilium*, Vatican II, 1963, no. 123

Ordinaries must be very careful to see that sacred furnishings and works of value are not disposed of or allowed to deteriorate; for they are the house of God.

—*Sacrosanctum Concilium*, Vatican II, 1963, no. 126

The Church through the centuries has also safeguarded the artistic treasures belonging to it. Accordingly, in our own times as well, bishops, no matter how hard pressed by their responsibilities, must take seriously the care of places of worship and sacred objects. They bear singular witness to the reverence of the people toward God and deserve such care also because of their historic and artistic value.

It grieves the faithful to see that more than ever before there is so much unlawful transfer of ownership of the historical and artistic heritage of the Church, as well as theft, confiscation, and destruction.

Disregarding the warnings and legislation of the Holy See, many people have made unwarranted changes in places of worship under the pretext of carrying out the reform of the liturgy and have thus caused the disfigurement or loss of priceless works of art. Mindful of the legislation of Vatican Council II and of the directives in the documents of the Holy See, bishops are to exercise unfailing vigilance to ensure that the remodeling of places of worship by reason of the reform of the liturgy is carried out with the utmost caution.

—*Opera Artis,*
Sacred Congregation of the Clergy, 1971, no. 4

Should it become necessary to adapt works of art and the treasures of the past to new liturgical laws, bishops are to take care that the need is genuine and that no harm comes to the work of art... When it is judged that any such works are no longer suited to divine worship, they are never to be given over to profane use. Rather they are to be set up in a fitting place, namely in a diocesan or interdiocesan museum, so that they are accessible to all who wish to look at them.

—*Opera Artis,*
Sacred Congregation of the Clergy, 1971, no. 6

Precious objects, especially votive offerings, are not to be disposed of without permission of the Holy See, in keeping with CIC can. 1532 (1917 *Code of Canon Law*). The penalties in can. 2347-2349 continue to apply to those transferring ownership of such objects unlawfully; such persons cannot be absolved until they have made restitution for the losses incurred.

—*Opera Artis,*
Sacred Congregation of the Clergy, 1971, no. 7

...all the churches should be given a definite arrangement which respects any artistic monuments, adapting them as far as possible to present day needs.
—Third Instruction on the Correct Implementation of the Constitution on Sacred Liturgy, Congregation for Divine Worship, 1970

Ordinary concern for preservation and appropriate security measures are to be used to protect sacred and precious goods.
—Code of Canon Law,1994, can. 1220 §2

Church art

Let bishops carefully exclude from the house of God and from other sacred places those works of artists which are repugnant to faith, morals, and Christian piety, and which offend true religious sense either by their distortion of forms or by lack of artistic worth, by mediocrity or by pretense.
*—Sacrosanctum Concilium,*Pope Paul VI,1963, no. 124

The practice of placing sacred images in churches so that they may be venerated by the faithful is to be maintained. Nevertheless their number should be moderate and their relative positions should reflect right order."
—Sacrosanctum Concilium, Pope Paul VI,1963, no. 125

Those decrees, which were given in the early days regarding the cult images of Christ, the Blessed Virgin and the saints [are to] be religiously observed."
—Lumen Gentium, Pope Paul VI,1964, no. 67

Arrangement of a Church

The sanctuary should be marked off from the nave by a higher floor level or by a distinctive structure and décor.
— *General Instruction of the Roman Missal*, 1973, no. 258

Worship of the Eucharist

The Eucharist is "the source and summit of the Christian life."(*Lumen Gentium* 11) "The other sacraments, and indeed all ecclesiastical ministries and works of the apostolate, are bound up with the Eucharist and are oriented toward it. For in the Eucharist is contained the whole spiritual good of the Church, namely Christ himself, our Pasch." (*Presbyterorum ordinis* 5)
—*Catechism of the Catholic Church*, 1994, no. 1324

Prayer of adoration in the presence of the Blessed Sacrament unites the faithful with the paschal mystery; it enables them to share in Christ's sacrifice, of which the Eucharist is the permanent sacrament.
—Pope John Paul II,
"Letter on the 750th anniversary of the Feast of Corpus Christi," no. 3

Jesus waits for us in this sacrament of love. Let us be generous with our time in going to meet Him in adoration and in contemplation that is full of faith and ready to make reparation for the great faults and crimes of the world. May our adoration never cease.
—Pope John Paul II, *Dominicae Cenae*, 1980, no. 3

In the liturgy of the Mass we express our faith in the Real Presence of Christ under the species of bread and wine by, among other ways, genuflecting or bowing deeply as a sign of adoration of the Lord. "The Catholic Church has always offered and still offers to the sacrament of the Eucharist the cult of adoration, not only during Mass, but also outside of it, reserving the consecrated hosts with the utmost care, exposing them to the solemn veneration of the faithful, and carrying them in procession."(Paul VI, *Mysterium Fidei* 56)

—*Catechism of the Catholic Church*, 1994, no. 1378

The liturgy

The liturgy, like the Church, is intended to be hierarchical and polyphonic, respecting the different roles assigned by Christ and allowing all the different voices to blend in one great hymn of praise.

—Pope John Paul II,
Ad limina address to U.S. bishops, Oct. 9, 1998

In the earthly liturgy we take part in a foretaste of that heavenly liturgy which is celebrated in the holy city of Jerusalem toward which we journey as pilgrims, where Christ is sitting at the right hand of God, a minister of the holies and of the true tabernacle; we sing a hymn to the Lord's glory with all the warriors of the heavenly army; venerating the memory of the saints, we hope for some part and fellowship with them; we eagerly await the Savior, Our Lord Jesus Christ, until He, our life, shall appear and we too will appear with Him in glory.

—Pope Paul VI, *Sacrosanctum Concilium*, 1963, no. 8

Taking part in the Eucharistic Sacrifice, which is the fount and apex of the whole Christian life, they offer the divine Victim to God, and offer themselves along with It. Thus, both by the act of oblation and through holy Communion, all perform their proper part in this liturgical service, not, indeed, all in the same way but each in that way which is appropriate to himself.

—Pope Paul VI, *Lumen Gentium,* 1964, no. 11

The liturgical books approved by the competent authority are to be faithfully observed in the celebration of the sacraments; therefore no one on personal authority may add, remove or change anything in them.

—*Code of Canon Law,* 1983, can. 846

Antiquarianism

The liturgy of the early ages is most certainly worthy of all veneration. But ancient usage must not be esteemed more suitable or proper, either in its own right or in its significance for later times and new situations, on the simple ground that it carries the savor and aroma of antiquity... It is neither wise nor laudable to reduce everything to antiquity by every possible device. Thus, to cite some instances one would be straying from the straight path were he to wish the altar to be restored to its primitive table form; were he to want black excluded as a color for the liturgical vestments; were he to forbid the use of sacred images and statues in Churches; were he to order the crucifix so designed that the divine Redeemer's body shows no trace of His cruel sufferings; and lastly were he to disdain and reject polyphonic music or singing in parts, even where it comes to regulations issued by the Holy see... Unwise and mistaken is the zeal of one who in matters liturgical would go back to the rites and usage of antiquity, discarding the new patterns introduced by disposition of divine Providence to meet the changes of circumstances and situation."

—Pope Pius XII, *Mediator Dei,* 1947, no. 61-64

Church furnishings

According to the traditional practice of the Church and the meaning of the altar, the table of a fixed altar should be of natural stone, but any solid, becoming, and skillfully constructed material may be used with the approval of the conference of bishops."
—*General Instruction of the Roman Missal*, 1973, no. 263

According to church custom the table of a fixed altar is to be of stone, in fact of a single natural stone; nevertheless, even another material, worthy and solid, in the judgement of the conference of bishops also can be used. The supports or the foundation can be made of any material
—*Code of Canon Law*, 1983, can. 1236 §1

It is fitting to maintain the practice of enclosing relics in the altar or of placing them under the altar."
—*General Instruction of the Roman Missal*, 1973, no. 266

The altar, around which the Church is gathered in the celebration of the Eucharist, represents the two aspects of the same mystery: the altar of sacrifice and the table of the Lord.
— *Catechism of the Catholic Church*, 1994, no. 1383

Rights and Obligations of the Laity

The laity have the right, as do all Christians, to receive in abundance from their sacred pastors the spiritual goods of the Church, especially the assistance of the Word of God and the sacraments. Every layman should openly reveal to them his needs and desires with that freedom and confidence which befits a son of God and a brother in

Christ. as sons and daughters, brothers and sisters in Christ. An individual layman, by the reason of the knowledge, competence, or outstanding ability which he may enjoy, is permitted and sometimes even obliged to express his opinion on things which concern the good of the Church.

When occasions arise, let this be done through the agencies set up by the Church for this purpose. Let it always be done in truth, in courage, and in prudence, with reverence and charity toward those who by reason of their sacred office represent the person of Christ.

—*Lumen Gentium*, Pope Paul VI, 1964, no. 37

The Christian faithful are free to make known their needs, especially spiritual ones, and their desires to the pastors of the Church. In accord with the knowledge, competence, and preeminence which they possess, they have the right and even at times the duty to manifest to the sacred pastors their opinion on matters which pertain to the good of the Church, and they have a right to make their opinion known to the other Christian faithful, with due regard to the integrity of faith and morals and reverence toward their pastors, and with consideration for the common good and the dignity of persons.

—*Code of Canon Law*, 1983, can. 212

SECTION 2
Other Useful Notes and Quotes

"Environment and Art in Catholic Worship"

Mistakes surfaced in [EACW]... 'Environment and Art,' in essence, relegated the Eucharist to a closet.[152]

—Francis Cardinal George
Archbishop of Chicago

The document says very little about the exterior of the church, its signification as a 'domus ecclesiae,' and its appropriate siting in the city or the country. There is no recognition of the scriptural metaphors of the city set on a hill, the lamp on a lampstand or the city of God. The ability of the church building to symbolize the Christian community and her belief in Christ, through domes, spires, bells, generous portals, atriums, gardens, and iconography is ignored."[153]

—Duncan G. Stroik
Professor of Architecture, University of Notre Dame

The Real Presence

Sacrosanctum Concilium, the Constitution on the Liturgy of the Second Vatican Council makes this clear in its famous reflection on the different modes of Christ's presence at Mass. "Holy Communion and Worship of the Eucharist Outside Mass" expands on this passage: In the

---

[152] Hitchcock, Helen Hull, "Bishops Mull Restructuring," *Adoremus Bulletin*, February, 1999.
[153] Stroik, Duncan G., "Environment and Art in Catholic Worship: A Critique," *Sacred Architecture*, Summer, 1999.

celebration of Mass the chief ways in which Christ is present in His Church gradually become clear. First he is present in the very assembly of the faithful, gathered together in His name; next He is present in His word, when the Scriptures are read in the Church and explained; then in the person of the minister; finally and above all, in the Eucharistic sacrament. In a way that is completely unique, the whole and entire Christ, God and man, is substantially and permanently present in the Sacrament. This presence of Christ under the appearance of bread and wine "is called real, not to exclude other kinds of presence as if they were not real, but because it is real par excellence." [154]

—Father James Moroney
Executive Director, Bishops' Committee on Liturgy

The Tabernacle

The place where the Blessed Sacrament is reserved should be very evident to the faithful, and "a special lamp to indicate and honor the presence of Christ is to burn at all times before the tabernacle in which the Most Holy Eucharist is reserved" (Can. no. 940). Visits to the Blessed Sacrament, before and after Mass and on other private occasions, should be encouraged as a way of preparing for the celebration of the Eucharist and of extending its meaning.

The traditional Catholic practice of genuflecting upon entering and leaving the church, and when passing in front of the Blessed Sacrament, should be maintained, as an

---

[154] Moroney, Fr. James, excerpt from an address given to the clergy of the Archdiocese of St. Louis at a symposium on Adoration of the Blessed Sacrament, February 2, 1998. Father Moroney is the director of the bishops' Committee on Liturgy.

external sign of our awareness of and respect for Christ" presence.[155]

—Bishop Thomas J. Tobin
Bishop of Youngstown

The pastors of the archdiocese already know my concern about the location of the Blessed Sacrament in our own churches. In new renovations permission is not granted to locate the tabernacle in a place where it is not visible by the great majority of the congregation. Most of our Catholic people can come into the church only for Sunday Mass. It would be a great loss for all of us if they were never conscious of the fact that the Lord is there reserved in the tabernacle for their adoration and their prayer. If they can never see the tabernacle, then their devotion to the Blessed Sacrament may soon begin to falter and decline.[156]

—Archbishop Theodore McCarrick,
Archbishop of Newark

Considerable discussion continues concerning the location of the tabernacle. However, all the official instructions during and since the Second Vatican Council need to be interpreted in light of Canon 938.2 of the Code of Canon Law, 1983: "The tabernacle in which the blessed Eucharist is reserved should be sited in a distinguished place in a church or oratory, a place which is conspicuous, suitably adorned and conducive to prayer."...

Studying the development within these directives, we see first of all that *Inaestimabile Donum* [1980] modifies the favor for a separate eucharistic chapel in GIRM, no. 276. In the decade separating the two instructions, problems had

---

[155] Tobin, Bishop Thomas J., *The Eucharist: To Be Loved, To Be Lived*, 1998.
[156] McCarrick, Archbishop Theodore, "All Praise and All Thanksgiving: A Pastoral Letter on the Eucharist, *Religious Life*, October, 1995.

arisen with a diminution of devotion to the Eucharist, not dissociated from inadequate attention to the place of reservation in new or renovated churches. This may explain why Canon 938.2 seems to reflect the mind of *Inaestimabile Donum* more than GIRM and the instructions on eucharistic worship. Canon 938.2 is not a mere synthesis of previous instructions. It corrects misinterpretations of those rules... We also see that locating a tabernacle on an altar always remains a valid option and is nowhere ruled out.[157]

—Msgr. Peter J. Elliot
Ceremonies of the Modern Roman Rite, 1995

"[T]here exists no mandate, in the primary sense of the term as a command or an order, to move the tabernacle from the high altar to another position in the church. With respect to the placement of the tabernacle, the instruction *Inter Oecumenici* (1964) par. 95, which implemented the decisions of *Sacrosanctum Consilium*, states quite clearly that the Blessed Sacrament be reserved on the high altar, a possibility envisaged also by *Eucharisticum Mysterium* (1967), par. 54... It is certainly true that a great number of churches since the Second Vatican Council have been rearranged; such changes, while inspired by the liturgical reform, cannot, however, be said to have been required by the legislation of the Church."[158]

—Cardinal Joseph Ratzinger,
Prefect for the Congregation for the Doctrine of the Faith

The tabernacle's function is as an extension of the Mass. Our personal prayer of adoration before the Blessed Sacrament is in continuity with the Mass, in participation with it, in desire if we cannot go. What Christ is doing in

---

[157] Elliot, Msgr. Peter J., *Ceremonies of the Modern Roman Rite*, San Francisco: Ignatius Press, 1995, page 872.
[158] Caesar, Bernard, "Cardinal Ratzinger on the Question of Sanctuary Renovations," *AD2000*, October, 1998.

the tabernacle is offering himself to the Father, just as in the Mass, and also wanting to nourish us in spiritual communion. He does something in the tabernacle, but it is in relation with the Mass.[159]

—Abbot Boniface Luykx
Vatican II peritus

Frankly, I have never met an adult Catholic who was ever confused about celebration [of the Holy Sacrifice of the Mass] at the expense of reservation or vice versa. Centrally located and recognizable tabernacles never contributed to such confusion; indeed, where a recognizable tabernacle is visible it is immediately obvious to all that it is for reservation only!"[160]

—Msgr. William Smith
Professor, St. Joseph's Seminary, NY

Adoration

Some have maintained that the promotion of the adoration of the Blessed Sacrament will take away from the centrality of the Eucharistic celebration. It need not do so. In fact, proper devotion to the Blessed Sacrament will inevitably lead to a fuller participation in the Eucharistic celebration: 'Outside the Eucharistic celebration, the Church is careful to venerate the Blessed Sacrament, which must be reserved... as the spiritual center of the religious and parish community. Contemplation prolongs communion and enables one to meet Christ, true God and true man, in a lasting way.[161]

—Bishop Thomas J. Tobin, Bishop of Youngstown

---

[159] Rt. Rev. Archimandrite Boniface Luykx, "Liturgical Architecture: Domus Dei or Domus Ecclesiae," *Catholic Dossier*, May-June, 1997.

[160] Smith, Msgr. William Smith, "Placement of the Tabernacle," *Homiletic & Pastoral Review*, December, 1998.

[161] Tobin, Bishop Thomas J., *The Eucharist: To Be Loved, To Be Lived*, 1998.

Iconoclasm

There are... a few things that must be kept in mind to prevent even greater iconoclasm in this country.

1.) The liturgy reforms of Vatican II did not intend the destruction of our churches or altars. Rather the new directions for the ceremonies of Mass and office were given with altars in the same sanctuary considered theologically or artistically proper.

2.) But the destruction of our churches will go down in history along with the iconoclasts of former eras. The Vatican Council never intended to destroy true art, but rather to foster it and preserve it.

3.) We must be warned against mere opinions being passed off as ecclesiastical law or the will of our bishops. It must be clear by whose authority further changes are mandated. We fortunately have learned from the sad experiences of the past. The laity, more than the clergy, have suffered as they have witnessed the abuse of their heritage and the sacrifices made by their forebears to create a decent place of worship. In their trust they accepted the directions of their pastors with reverence and obedience. Unfortunately too often the parish clergy were in ignorance of the liturgical laws and as a result they had foisted on them these aberrations which have so disillusioned a whole generation of Catholics, whose faith has been sorely tested. In too many instances people have failed the test, and have been driven out of the Church they knew and loved.

4.) Our bishops are our masters in liturgical renewal. They alone, with the approval of the Holy See, can determine what and how the liturgy is to be celebrated. They have spoken through the documents of the Second Vatican Council, which, together with the papal and curial statements since the closing of the Council, direct us and we must obey. There are some who do not wish to accept what has been given us, but rather have their own ideas which they try to promote by publishing them as if they were authoritative. Advisory boards are perfectly in order and wise, but they merely report their findings and suggestions to the committee that called them into being, and that committee in turn reports to the general body of bishops for a vote, which requires a certain majority and finally the approval of the Holy See. Both in the area of art and that of music, the clergy and laity have been led along by opinions passed off as authoritative documents.

5.) Finally, ask why these changes are being proposed and even demanded. Certainly there is ignorance of the liturgical law on the part of the clergy, and many priests depended on information solely on the directions of their bishops, many of whom in their turn are dependent on their advisors, who further in turn have accepted too much of the propaganda that has emanated from the national headquarters in Washington.[162]

—Monsignor Richard Schuler,
Pastor, St. Agnes Church, St. Paul, Minn.

Arrangement of Churches

The whole church should be arranged so as to invite adoration and contemplation even where there are no celebrations. One must long to frequent it in order to meet the Lord there... The Church, by its beautiful liturgical layout, its tabernacle radiating Christ's real presence, should be the beautiful house of the Lord and of His Church, where the faithful love to recollect themselves in the silence of adoration and contemplation. Every church must be "praying" even when no liturgical celebrations are

---

[162] Schuler, Msgr. Richard, *Adoremus Bulletin*, April, 1997. Msgr. Schuler is President of the Church Music Association of America and is a former editor of *Sacred Music*.

taking place; it must be a place where in a restless world, one can meet the Lord in peace.[163]

—*Max Thurian*
L'Osservatore Romano

Church renovators

When specialists in church remodeling enter a venerable structure, remove the side altars, most of the statues, and the communion rail, replace the high altar with a communion table, and relocate the tabernacle to some place where it is hardly noticeable, they are consciously exorcising the parishioners' sense of sacred space. Their intention is that in time Catholics should lose that sense, as the palpable vandalism (as many people see it) done to their buildings itself serves to demystify the structures.

When speaking candidly, liturgists now admit that in an ideal situation there would be no church building at all, merely a meeting space suitable for a variety of uses, of which formal worship is only one. They content themselves with systematically stripping existing churches only because it is not feasible to destroy them completely.[164]

—*James Hitchcock*
Professor of History, St. Louis University

One of the most influential church renovators is John Buscemi, an ex-Franciscan priest from Loyola University in Chicago, who has traveled throughout the United States piping his "new ecclesiology of the visual — and leaving path of broken churches and divided congregations in his wake. Like the Pied Piper, who was employed by the leaders

---

[163] Thurian, Max, *L'Osservatore Romano*, July 21, 1996.
[164] Hitchcock, James, "Saint Nowhere's," *Catholic Dossier*, May-June, 1997, page 60. Dr. Hitchcock is professor of history at St. Louis University. He is the author of numerous books, including *Recovery of the Sacred*.

of Hamlin but emptied the town of what it held most dear, Buscemi has the official sanction of parish leaders or liturgy committees. Like the Piper, his power seems virtually irresistible, as many parishioners attest who protested in vain and mourn over their bare ruined choirs.

Buscemi may not reveal to the parish groups he addresses his real reasons for wanting to remove statues, kneelers, altar rails, stained glass, and the corpus from crucifixes, nor why the walls must be stripped of images of saints. But he does not conceal his motives in his writings. In a recent tract called "Places for Devotion," he says that specific images, especially the image of the crucified Christ on the cross, are too limiting. The cross, he says, is really a transcultural symbol of paradox, "resolved" at the point of crossing, which should be an open space — a "birth canal" through which the spirit can freely pass.[165]

—*Helen Hull Hitchcock*
Editor, Adoremus Bulletin

I believe that these men and women are imprisoned in the recent past because they cling to a kind of 'Maoist' mythology of a perpetual or 'ongoing' liturgical revolution. That mythology is derived from a dated commitment to a permanent program of planned changes rather than to organic and natural development. It has not made these people popular within the wider Church, which they do not always understand."[166]

—*Msgr. Peter J. Elliot*
Author, Ceremonies of the Modern Roman Rite

---

[165] Hitchcock, Helen Hull, "The New Barbarians," *Catholic Dossier*, May-June 1997, page 62. Mrs. Hitchcock is editor of the liturgical journal *Adoremus Bulletin*.

[166] Elliot, Msgr. Peter J., *Liturgical Question Box*, San Francisco: Ignatius Press, 1998, page 16.

CHAPTER 6

References and Resources for Further Research
Recommended Architects, Books, Journals, and Essays

80C8

Church documents

THE FOLLOWING IS a bibliography of authoritative Church documents that address in some way matters of church architecture, design or renovation. Useful for parishioners, pastors, building committee members and architects, these documents present the Church's teaching on church art and architecture.

Divini Cultus, Apostolic Constitution on Divine Worship, Pope Pius XI, 1928.

Mediator Dei, Encyclical on the Sacred Liturgy, Pope Pius XII, 1947.

Sacrosanctum Concilium, Vatican II's The Constitution on the Sacred Liturgy, 1963.

Sacram Liturgiam, Motu Proprio on the Sacred Liturgy, Pope Paul VI, 1964.

Inter Oecumenici, Instruction on the Proper Implementation of the Constitution on the Sacred Liturgy, approved by Pope Paul VI, 1964.

Tres Abhinc Annos, Second Instruction on the Proper Implementation of the Constitution on the Sacred Liturgy, approved by Pope Paul VI, 1967.

Eucharisticum Mysterium, Instruction on the Worship of the Eucharistic Mystery, Pope Paul VI, 1967.

Liturgicae Instaurationes, Third Instruction on the Correct Implementation of the Constitution on the Sacred Liturgy, Pope Paul VI, 1970.

Opera Artis, Circular Letter on the Care of the Church's Historical and Artistic Heritage, Sacred Congregation for the Clergy, approved by Pope Paul VI, 1971.

Eucharistiae Sacramentum, On Holy Communion and the Worship of the Eucharist Outside of Mass, Pope Paul VI, 1973.

Dedication of a Church and an Altar, Sacred Congregation for Divine Worship, 1977.

Dominicae Cenae, On the Mystery and Worship of the Eucharist, Pope John Paul II, 1980.

Inaestimabile Donum, Instruction on Certain Norms Concerning the Worship of the Eucharistic Mystery, Sacred Congregation for Divine Worship (approved by Pope John Paul II), 1980.

Code of Canon Law, approved by Pope John Paul II, 1983.

Duodecimum Saeculum, On representations and imagery, Pope John Paul II, 1987.

Love Your Mass, Apostolic Letter on the 25th anniversary of *Sacrosanctum Concilium,* Pope John Paul II, 1988.

Catechism of the Catholic Church, approved by Pope John Paul II, 1994.

Ecclesiae de Mysterio, On certain questions regarding the collaboration of the non-ordained faithful in the sacred ministry of priests, approved by Pope John Paul II, 1997.

Apostolos Suos, On the limitations of national episcopal conferences, Pope John Paul II, 1998.

Letter to Artists, Pope John Paul II, 1999.

Resources on church architecture

This section provides a list of journals, articles, books and websites pertaining to church architecture and relevant liturgical matters. The church architecture of the present and future ought to, in the words of *Sacrosanctum Concilium,* "grow organically from forms already existing." The resources including in this section serve as visual and textual sources for church architecture. Most of these do not require special education or technical knowledge to make them useful for new church design or renovation. Many of the books provide an excellent array of images that explain the various traditional arrangements of churches. Others provide a sampling of beautiful 20th century churches that can be used for inspiring church designs of the 21st century.

RECOMMENDED JOURNALS:

Sacred Architecture
3 issues a year, $12.95 (plus $5.00 outside the U.S.)
Sacred Architecture
P.O. Box 556
Notre Dame IN 46556
Editor: Duncan Stroik, associate professor of architecture
at Notre Dame
Phone: (219)631-5762,
Email: dstroik@nd.edu

Sacred Architecture, the journal of the Institute for Sacred Architecture, examines issues of tradition and innovation in new church design and includes critiques of new churches and Catholic buildings as well as news, theory, and book reviews.

According to editor Duncan Stroik, *Sacred Architecture* is partially a response to the numerous requests he has received from Catholic pastors and laity for information and advice on church design and evaluation of available church architects. In an introductory editorial he writes that such requests indicate a need for "an architectural publication which will draw on the riches of the Catholic patrimony and articulate the principles for a sacramental architecture."

He notes that while most major Catholic journals include criticism of contemporary film, drama, music and art, surprisingly little attention is paid in their pages to contemporary church architecture. By sponsoring "substantive debate about sacred architecture" in a journal "committed to the promotion of the cultural heritage of the Church," Professor Stroik hopes to address "a sudden awareness that what we have been praying in for the past few decades has not measured up."

Adoremus Bulletin
P.O. Box 3286
St. Louis, MO 63130
(314) 863 – 8385
Editor: Mrs. Helen Hull Hitchcock
Website: http://www.adoremus.org
Email: editor@adoremus.org

The *Bulletin* is the monthly publication of Adoremus, the Society for the Renewal of the Sacred Liturgy, an association of Catholics established to promote authentic reform of the liturgy of the Roman Rite.

The mission of Adoremus is to rediscover and restore the beauty, the holiness, the power of the Church's rich liturgical tradition while remaining faithful to an organic, living process of renewal.

Adoremus fully and unreservedly accepts the Second Vatican Council as an act of the Church's supreme Magisterium (teaching authority) guided by the Holy Spirit, and regards its documents as an expression, in our time, of the word of Christ himself for His Bride, the Church.

Adoremus' guiding principle for authentic liturgical reform is enunciated in *Sacrosanctum Concilium*, §23: "...there must be no innovations unless the good of the Church genuinely and certainly requires them, and care must be taken that any new form adopted should in some way grow organically from forms already existing."

The *Adoremus Bulletin* has been publishing insightful and informative articles on the subject of church art and architecture, among many other liturgical issues, since 1995.

Christifidelis
Newsletter for the St. Joseph Foundation
11107 Wurzbach #601B
San Antonio TX 78230-2553

Director: Charles M. Wilson
Phone: (210) 697-0717
Website: http://www.st-joseph-foundation.org

Christifidelis is the newsletter for the St. Joseph Foundation, a non-profit organization that provides canonical assistance to both priests and laity. The foundation was founded shortly after the promulgation of the 1983 Code of Canon Law, to aid the faithful in fighting abuses in the Church. Most of the abuses complained of by faithful Catholics, reports Foundation director Charles M. Wilson, appear to be violations of their right to the spiritual goods of the Church (canon 213), their right to worship according to the lawful norms (canon 214), their right to a [truly] Christian education (canon 217) and their right to seek, embrace and keep the truth in the matters which concern God and His Church (canon 748).

The foundation has aided hundreds of Catholics across the country to appeal abusive and unjust renovation processes and proposals throughout the country. The newsletter keeps readers up-to-date on current canonical issues regarding church renovations (among a host of others topics), and chronicles some of the fights along the way.

St. Catherine Review
6 issues a year, $20 (plus $10 outside the U.S.)
P.O. Box 11260
Cincinnati OH 45211-0260
Editor: Michael S. Rose
Phone: (513) 661-7009
Email: stcate@erinet.com
Website: http://www.aquinas-multimedia.com/catherine

St. Catherine Review is a bi-monthly journal of Catholic issues. For the past few years it has chronicled several church renovation projects that provide illustrative material for much of what is addressed in this book. The Review's website includes an archive of writings on church architecture, as well as many other topics that would be of interest to Catholics across the country. It also includes reviews of church architecture.

The Catholic Liturgical Library
Website: http://www.catholicliturgy.com
Editor: Ian Rutherford
Email: webmaster@catholicliturgy.com

The Catholic Liturgical Library is dedicated to providing accurate historical and current information about the liturgies of the Latin (Roman) rite of the Catholic Church. It is the most comprehensive collection on the World Wide Web of authoritative documentation regarding the liturgy, church architecture and art, sacred music, and rubrics. It also includes reprints of helpful and informative articles, book reviews, periodical reviews and transcripts from liturgical conferences. Perhaps its most helpful section is the Church documents. It includes the full text for the *General Instruction of the Roman Missal*, Vatican II and post-conciliar documents pertaining to various aspects of liturgy—a great resource.

Editor Ian Rutherford also issues an electronic newsletter, *The Liturgical Chronicle*, available via email. To subscribe to that free service, email Ian at the above address.

Recent Essays and Articles

Brouse, Michael. "A Young Emperor's Gift: St. Bartholomew on the Tibre Island," *Inside the Vatican*, May, 1998.

Carey, Ann. "Renovated, Restored... Renewed!" *Adoremus Bulletin*, July/Aug., 1998.

Delarue, Anthony. "Liturgical Architecture: Its Abuse and Restoration," *Sursum Corda*, Winter, 1999.

Dimock, O.P., Giles. "Will Beauty Look After Herself?" *Sacred Music*, Fall, 1990.

Dimock, O.P., Giles. "Why We Need Beautiful Churches," *New Oxford Review*, June, 1997.

Dimock, O.P., Giles. "The Beauty of God's House," *Catholic Dossier*, May/June, 1997.

Elliot, Msgr. Peter J. "Where should we put the tabernacle?" *Adoremus Bulletin*, Dec. 97/Jan., 1998.

Enright, Fr. Michael. "No cheap churches," *Crisis*, November, 1996.

Galles, Duane L.C.M. "God's Dwelling Place," *Laywitness*, October, 1999.

Galles, Duane L.C.M. "Locating a Tabernacle," *Christifidelis*, August 10, 1999.

Galles, Duane L.C.M. "Canonical Basics: Questions about the Tabernacle," *Christifidelis*, August 10, 1999.

Hardinge Menzies, Henry. "What Happened to the Glory," *Catholic Position Papers*, No. 235, January, 1995.

Hitchcock, Helen Hull. "The New Barbarians: Cactus in the Chancel," *Catholic Dossier*, May/June, 1997.

Hitchcock, Helen Hull. "They have taken away my lord, and I know not where they laid him," *Adoremus Bulletin*, July/Aug, 1999.

Hitchcock, Helen Hull. "What's the Real Story on EACW?" *Adoremus Bulletin,* June, 1999.

Hitchcock, James. "St. Nowhere's," *Catholic Dossier,* May/June, 1997.

Mannion, Msgr. M. Francis. "Ten Theses on a Church Door," *National Catholic Register,* March 2-8, 1997.

McNamara, Dennis R. "Can we keep our churches Catholic?" *Adoremus Bulletin,* March, 1998.

McNamara, Dennis R. "Church Architecture and Decorum," *Homiletic and Pastoral Review,* April, 1998.

McNamara, Dennis R. "So, You're on the Parish Building Committee," *Adoremus Bulletin,* February, 1999.

Rose, Michael S. "The Gothic Ideal and Modern Church Architecture," *Homiletic & Pastoral Review,* July, 1998.

Rose, Michael S. "Can Modern Churches Be Beautiful?" *National Catholic Register,* June 13-19, 1999.

Rose, Michael S. "Church Renovator Thrives on Manipulation Skills," *The Wanderer,* April 1, 1999.

Rose, Michael S. "Resistance to a Renovation," *The Wanderer,* September 9, 1999.

Rose, Michael S. "Notre Dame: Renovation Redux," *Adoremus Bulletin,* October, 1999.

Ruse, Austin. "Risen from the Ashes," *Sursum Corda,* Summer, 1998.

Schönborn, O.P., Christophe Cardinal. "The Temple as the Maternal Place of the Church," *Catholic Dossier,* May/June, 1997.

Smith, Thomas Gordon. "An Architecture to Honor the Church's Vision," *Adoremus Bulletin,* November, 1997.

Smith, Thomas Gordon. "Reconnecting to Tradition," *Sursum Corda,* Fall, 1998.

Smith, Msgr. William. "Place of the Tabernacle," *Homiletic & Pastoral Review,* December, 1998.

Stroik, Duncan. "Environment and Art in Catholic Worship: A Critique," *Sacred Architecture,* Summer, 1999.

Stroik, Duncan. "The Roots of Modernist Architecture," *Adoremus Bulletin,* October, 1997.

Stroik, Duncan. "Modernist Church Architecture," *Catholic Dossier,* May/June, 1997.

Stroik, Duncan. "Ten Myths of Contemporary Church Architecture," *Sacred Architecture,* Fall, 1998.

Stroik, Duncan. "Environment and Art in Catholic Worship: A Critique," *Sacred Architecture,* Summer, 1999.

Worden, William. "Renovation of Churches," *Sacred Music,* Spring, 1990.

BOOKS

Adams, Henry. *Mont-Saint-Michel and Chartres*. Cambridge, MA: The Riverside Press, 1904.

Anson, Peter. *Churches, Their Plan and Furnishing*. Milwaukee, WI: Bruce Publishing Co., 1948.

Aubert, Marcel. *French Cathedral Windows*. New York: Oxford University Press, 1947.

Borromeo, St. Charles. *Instructions on Ecclesiastical Buildings*. Evelyn Carol Voelker, translator. Dissertation, Syracuse University, 1979.

Brannach, Frank. *Church Architecture: Building for A Living Faith*, 1932.

Collins, Msgr. Harold E. *The Church Edifice and Its Appointments*, 1925.

Comes, John T. *Catholic Art and Architecture: A Lecture to Seminarists*, 1920.

Conant, Kenneth John. *Carolingian and Romanesque Architecture 800-1200*. Baltimore, MD: Penguin Books, 1959.

Conover, Elbert. *Building the House of God*, 1928.

Conover, Elbert. *The Church Builder*, 1930.

Conover, Elbert. *Planning Church Building*, 1945.

Conover, Elbert. *Building for Worship*, 1945.

Conover, Elbert. *The Church Building Guide*, 1946.

Cram, Ralph Adams. *Church Building*. Boston, MA: Marshall Jones Co., 1924.

Cram, Ralph Adams. *The Ministry of Art*, 1914.

Cram, Ralph Adams. *American Church Building of Today*, 1929.

Didron, Alphonse Napoleon. *Christian Iconography: The History of Christian Art in the Middle Ages* (2 volumes). New York: Fredrick Ungar Publishing Co., 1965.

Elliot, Msgr. Peter J. *Ceremonies of the Modern Roman Rite*. San Francisco: Ignatius Press, 1995.

Elliot, Msgr. Peter J. *Liturgical Question Box*. San Francisco: Ignatius Press, 1998.

Fletcher, Sir Banister. *A History of Architecture on the Comparative Method*. London: B.T. Batsford Ltd.,1896.

Frankl, Paul. *Gothic Architecture*. Baltimore, MD: Penguin Books, 1967.

Gill, Eric. *Beauty Looks After Herself*. London: Sheed & Ward, 1933.

Grabar, Andre. *Christian Iconography: A Study of Its Origins*. Princeton, NJ: Princeton University Press, 1968.

Grodecki, Louis. *Gothic Architecture*. New York: Abrams, 1976.

Hammett, Ralph Warner. *The Romanesque Architecture of Western Europe*. New York: The Architectural Book Publishing Co., 1927.

Jones, E. Michael. *Living Machines*. San Francisco: Ignatius Press, 1995.

Kraus, Henry. *The Living Theatre of Medieval Art*. Bloomington, IN: Indiana University Press, 1967.

Krautheimer, Richard. *Early Christian and Byzantine Architecture*. Baltimore, MD: Penguin Books, 1965.

Kubach, Hans Erich. *Romanesque Architecture*. New York: Abrams, 1972.

Kubler, George and Soria, Martin. *Art and Architecture in Spain and Portugal 1500- 1800*. Baltimore, MD: Penguin Books, 1959.

Lee, Lawrence; Seldon, George; and Stephens, Francis. *Stained Glass*. New York: Crown Publishers, Inc., 1976.

Lowrie, Walter. *Art in the Early Church*. New York: Pantheon Books, 1947.

Mango, Cyril. *Byzantine Architecture*. New York: Abrams, 1974.

Martindale, Andrew. *Gothic Art From the Twelfth to Fifteenth Century*. New York: Fredrick A. Praeger, Inc. Publishers, 1967.

Mitchel, Ann. *Cathedrals of Europe*. Norwich, UK: Hanlyn Publishing Group Limited, 1968.

Murray, Peter. *Renaissance Architecture*. New York: Abrams, 1971.

Norberg-Schulz, Christian. *Late Baroque and Rococo Architecture*. New York: Abrams, 1971.

Onians, John, *Bearers of Meaning*, 1988.

Portoghesi, Paolo. *The Rome of Borromini: Architecture as Language*. New York: George Braziller, Inc., 1967.

Roulin, Dom E. *Modern Church Architecture*, 1947.

Schloeder, Steven J. *Architecture in Communion*. San Francisco: Ignatius Press, 1998.

Short, Ernest. ed. *Post War Church Building: A Practical Handbook*. London: Hollis and Carter, 1947.

Smith, Thomas Gordon. *Classical Architecture: Rule and Invention*. Layton, UT: G.M. Smith, 1988.

Stoddard, Whitney S. *The West Portals of Saint-Denis and Chartres*. Cambridge, MA: Harvard University Press, 1952.

Suger, Abbot. *The Abbey Church of St.-Denis and Its Art Treasures*. E. Panofsky, translator. Princeton, NJ: Princeton University Press, 1979.

Tapie, Victor-L. *The Age of Grandeur: Baroque Art and Architecture*. New York: Grove Press, Inc., 1957.

Temco, Allen. *Notre-Dame of Paris: The Biography of a Cathedral*. New York: The Viking Press, 1955.

Volbach, W.F. *Early Christian Art.*   New York: Harry N. Abrams, Inc., (no date).

Von Simson, Otto. *The Gothic Cathedral: Origins of Gothic Architecture and the Medieval Concept of Order.* New York: Harper & Row, 1964.

Webb, Geoffrey. *Architecture in Britain: The Middle Ages.* Baltimore, MD: Penguin Books, Inc., 1956.

Weber, Edward J. *Catholic Church Buildings: Their Planning and Furnishing,* 1927.

Wilson, Christopher. *The Gothic Cathedral: The Architecture of the Great Church 1130- 1530.* London: Thames and Hudson Ltd., 1990.

Wittkower, Rudolf. *Art and Architecture in Italy 1600-1750.* Baltimore, MD: Penguin Books, 1958.

Recommended Architects and Artists

Oftentimes, through either ignorance or a desire to accommodate inauthentic liturgical fads, architects cannot or do not know how to build appropriate Catholic churches. This section provides a concise list of some architects who understand the Church's architectural patrimony and are committed to traditional Catholic church architecture as outlined in the present work. This ought to be an excellent resource for dioceses and parish building committees when it comes time to find an architect. North American and European architects are included.

Two architects especially recommended are Thomas Gordon Smith and Duncan Stroik from the University of Notre Dame School of Architecture.

North American

Mr. Duncan G. Stroik
University of Notre Dame
School of Architecture
110 Bond Hall
Notre Dame IN 46556
(219) 271-0522 — office
(219) 631-5762 — school
(219) 631-8486 — fax
Email: dstroik@nd.edu

Mr. Thomas Gordon Smith
2025 Edison Road
South Bend IN 46637
(219) 287-1498 — office
(219) 287-0821 — fax
(219) 631-6137 — school
(219) 631-8486 — fax

Mr. Angelo Alberto
3801 Kennett Pike, D
Wilmington, DE 19807
(302) 376-6450
(302) 376-6460 — fax
aatownplan@aol.com

Mr. H. Reed Armstrong
13 Sussex Road
Silver Spring MD 20910
(301) 585-4456
(301) 608-0532 — fax

Mr. John Blatteau
1930 Chestnut Street, #5
Philadelphia PA 19103
(215) 751-9779
(215) 751-0734 — fax
doric@pobox.upenn.edu

Mr. John Burgee, Architect
1592 E. Mountain Drive
Montecito CA 93108
(805) 969-5239 — tel/fax

Mr. Lio Casas and
Mr. Michael Mesko
Curtis and Windham
3701 Travis St.
Houston TX 77002

Mr. Andrés Duany and Mrs.
Elizabeth Plater-Zyberk
DPZ Architects
1023 SW 25th Ave.
Miami FL 33135
(305) 644-1023
(305) 644-102 — fax

Mr. Robert Goodall
1300 Spring St.
Silver Spring, MD 20910
(301) 588-4800

Mr. Henry Hardinge
Menzies, Architect
99 Overlook Circle
New Rochelle, NY 10804
(914) 235-0198
(914) 235-7805 — fax
Email: hmenzies@aol.com

Mr. William Heyer and
Mrs. Selena Heyer
125 West Marion St. #116
South Bend IN 46601
(219) 251-0649
(219) 287-0821

Mr. Carter Hord
80 Monroe #102
Memphis TN 38103
(901) 527-9085
(703) 739-3845
(703) 739-3846 — fax

Mr. Michael Imber
111 W. El Prado
San Antonio TX 78212
(210) 824-7703

Mr. Dennis H. Keefe
Keefe Associates, Inc.
162 Boylston St.
Boston, MA 02116
(617) 482-5859
(617) 482-7321 — fax

Mr. James Langley
Department of Fine Arts
Franciscan University
100 Franciscan Way
Steubenville, OH 43952
(614) 282-3904
(614) 283-6401 — fax

Mr. Dino Marcantonio
270 Lafayette St, #300
New York NY 10012
(212) 941-8088

Mr. James McCrery
625 East Capitol St. NE
Washington DC 20003
(205) 588-0700

Mr. Duncan McRoberts
150 Lake St. South, Ste 208
Kirkland, WA 98033

Mr. Paul Milana
Cooper Robertson Partners
311 West 43 Street
New York, NY 10036
(212) 247-1717
(212) 245-0361 — fax

Mr. Stefan Molina
Turner Boaz Stocker
301 N. Market St., Ste 200
Dallas TX 75206
(214) 761-9465

Mr. Edward Mudd
23 Park Place
New Canaan CT 06840

Mr. Kevin Roche
20 Davis St
Hamden CT 06517
(203) 777-7251
(203) 776-2299 fax

Mr. Steven Semes
Cooper Robertson Partners
311 West 43 Street
New York NY 10036
(212) 247-1717
(212) 245-0361 fax

Mr. John Tittmann
58 Winter St.
Boston, MA 02108
(617) 451-5740
(617) 451-2309 — fax
Email: artarch@wn.net

David Vatter, Architect
603 Olympia Rd.
Pittsburgh PA 15211
(412) 431-4245 — tel/fax

European/Asian

Pier Carlo Bontempi
Studio Bontempi Strada
Nazionale 96C
43030 Gaiano di Collecchio
ITALY
(011) 390-521-80-9900

Piotr Choynowski
B). Farmanns GT. MB
0271 Oslo
NORWAY
(011) 47-22-55-2114
(011) 47-22-566-9777
(011) 47-22-552-114 — fax

José Cornelio da Silva
Colares 2710 Sintra
PORTUGAL
(011) 3511-888-2657

Anthony Delarue Associates
22 Lonsdale Square
London N1 1EN
GREAT BRITAIN
(011) 0171-700-0241
(011) 0171-700-0242 — fax

Michael Fuchs
A-3400 Klosterneuberg
Hermannstrasse 12
AUSTRIA
(011) 43-2243-253-82
M.Fuchs@michael-fuchs.at

David Mayernik
Roma ITALY
(011) 39-06-689-2626
Email: jtmayernik@ibm.net

Jan Maciag
Maple Tree Cottage
New Road, Orton Waterville,
Peterborough PE2 5EJ
GREAT BRITAIN
(011) 440-1733-230816
(011) 440-1733-391661
113125.2240@compuserve.com

José Narciso
Asian Architects
Room 202 SEDCCO Bldg.
120 Rada St., Legaspi Vill.
Makati, Metro Manila
PHILIPPINES

Helmut Peuker
Ainmillerstrasse 25
80801 München
GERMANY

Cristiano Rosponi
Via Muzio Attendolo 65
00176 Roma
ITALY
(011) 39-06-214-8050
Email: roscri@ flashnet.it

INDEX

ABOUT THE AUTHOR

MICHAEL S. ROSE (b. 1969) holds degrees in Architecture and Fine Arts from the University of Cincinnati and Brown University. He worked as an intern architect in London, New York, San Francisco, Boston, and Baltimore before returning to Cincinnati.

Mr. Rose writes frequently on the subject of church architecture and the renovation process. His articles have appeared in numerous journals and newspapers such as *Homiletic & Pastoral Review, Adoremus Bulletin, Catholic World Report, Laywitness, Sacred Architecture, National Catholic Register,* and *The Wanderer.*

Mr. Rose edits *St. Catherine Review* and *St. Joseph Messenger* in Cincinnati, where he resides with his wife and three children.

He can be reached by email at: mrose@erinet.com.

ABOUT ST. CATHERINE REVIEW

For those who are interested in keeping abreast of the issues addressed in *The Renovation Manipulation,* you may want to subscribe to *St. Catherine Review,* a bi-monthly journal of Catholic issues edited by Michael S. Rose.

St. Catherine Review
P.O. Box 11260
Cincinnati OH 45211-0260

Subscriptions are $20/year

ജ∞ᚽ